Destiny

May Yen Ting

Translated By Amelia Fielden

Printed in the United States of America

Quadu Press
www.quadupress.com
quadupress@gmail.com

Editors
Ling-Erl Ting [丁玲兒]
Warren Wu [吳維倫]

Contents

Editor's Note

My mother, Ting Yen May [丁顏梅, Tei Gan Ume in Japanese], began writing *tanka* after retiring from teaching and after a chance reunion with her high school Japanese language teacher, Shiga Mitsuko-sensei [四賀光子先生], in 1971. Shiga-sensei not only guided and read my mother's drafts of *tanka* but also encouraged her to save her works and leave them as a keepsake for her descendants. This is mentioned in the afterword, and it made a deep impression on me when I first read *Destiny* forty years ago. Ever since then it has been on my mind to take up the task of translating her works into English so that I can pass on her keepsake gift to our next generation who are not proficient in Japanese. I am grateful to Amelia Fielden, an Australian poet and translator of Japanese literature, for her skillful and beautiful translation of *tanka* to naturally flowing *tanka* in English form. Also, my deep appreciation goes to Ogi Saeko-sama, *tanka* poet from Australia, and Maki Tomoe-sensei, a *tanka* poet and teacher at the Japanese Community Pioneer Center in Los Angeles, for their proof reading of *tanka* phrasing. The English version of *Destiny* is not only a keepsake for my next generation but also for those who are interested in studying *tanka* in Japanese and English forms.

Special thanks to my husband, Kai-Min Wu, who translated the introduction and the afterword, and to my son, Warren Wu, who did the detailed editing. Also, thanks to my sister-in-law, Kathy Ting, and my siblings, Joyce Marleau, Leland Ting, Elon Ting for their support.

Ling-Erl Ting
February 21, 2014

Figure 1 – Ting Yen May with Shiga Mitsuko-sensei.

Introduction

The author of this book, Ting Yen May [丁顏梅さん] started writing *tanka* as a special member of *Chō-On* [潮音] in the fall of 1971 with great enthusiasm. As Mrs. Ting mentions in the afterword, our relationship began while I was a teacher at Tokyo Prefectural First Girls' High School [東京府立第一高等女学校 (現白鷗高校)].

Mrs. Ting majored in liberal arts and graduated from Tokyo Women's Higher Normal College [東京女高師, now Ochanomizu University (現お茶の水大學)]. Therefore, she has a deep understanding of Japanese literature and poetry. Mrs. Ting even wrote textbooks for students in Taiwan to learn Japanese. With this background, the expression of her *tanka* is very accurate and proper. The Japanese language she learned so diligently while attending the highest level of academic institution was later designated a foreign language. Furthermore, her nationality was changed from Japanese to Chinese after World War II. Even today, Taiwan's national status is in question. The *tanka* she wrote under such circumstances resonate in our hearts.

I believe that Mrs. Ting's works will be valued greatly by those who ponder the subjects of nationality and international relations. For this reason, I encouraged her to publish this book and gladly see it is done.

Destiny follows the thoughts outlined above. I selected the *tanka* to be included, and Ōta Seikyū [太田青丘] edited them. There are 432 *tanka*, and it is worth mentioning that they are the work produced over the span of three and a half years.

I am substituting a more formal foreword with this brief introduction.

Shiga Mitsuko
April 1, 1975

1971

師のみ声

七月米国よりの帰途、東京府立第一高等女学校一年に在学当時の国文の師、四賀光子
先生に東京の帝国ホテルより始めて電話を差し上ぐ

レシーバーに
聞く師のみ声
爽やかに
八十六歳と
などか思はん

May Yen Ting

My Teacher's Voice

On my way back home from America in July, I made a call from the Imperial Hotel in Tokyo, ringing for the first time Shiga Mitsuko-sensei, who had been my year one teacher of Japanese literature when I studied at the Tokyo Prefectural First Girls' High School.

in the receiver

I hear my teacher's voice

so fresh and lively

how could I believe

her to be eighty-six

たらちねに
ま向ふ思ひ
師の君に
学びるし日は
五十年の過去

燈台の
灯と師の君を
仰ぎつつ
今日より後の
わが生はげまん

枕辺に
筆紙置きて
目覚めたる
夜半にも歌を
作らんと思ふ

歌の道
知らねど今は
我が思ひ
述べんとただに
心のはやる

it's as though I am
facing my beloved mother —
those days I learned from you,
honorable teacher,
are fifty years in the past

looking up to
my teacher as the light
from a lighthouse,
I will put more effort
into the rest of my life

placing pen and paper
by my pillow, I plan
to write tanka
when I wake,
even if it's midnight

although ignorant
of the way of tanka,
I am simply impatient,
wanting to express
my thoughts right now

久々に
筆擱きて物を
縫ひおれば
女我はも
心安らぐ

人生は
三十までと
嘯きし
我が若き日よ
アルバムを繰る

家族集ふ

七月ポートランド三男の家にて結婚四十周年の記念として全家族集まる

かにかくに
四十年共に
歩み来て
今日ここに聞く
子らの祝ぎ言

子も孫も
来て寿げば
四十年
この日の為に
我等生きしか

6

when at length

I set aside my pen

to do some sewing,

my womanly heart

is set at peace

in my young days

such wild talk

of living

until thirty—

I turn the pages of my album

The Family Gets Together

In July, the whole family gathered in Portland to celebrate our fortieth wedding anniversary at the home of our third son.

in one way or another

we have gone along together

for forty years—

here, today, we listen

to our children's congratulations

our children and grandchildren

have come to celebrate—

is it for this day

we have been living

the last forty years?

月下美人草

幾月の
営（いとな）みを夜の
ひと時に
咲き極まるや
月下美人の花

束（つか）の間の
花の命よ
月下美人
葉よりたわわに
咲き極まれる

息づきて
ある如き蕾
見るうちに
ふくらみて行く
月下美人草

咲き出づる
花の一途（いちづ）の
営みを
見つつ何時しか
息つめてゐぬ

The *Queen of the Night*: Night-blooming Cereus

after several months of work,
on a certain evening
at a certain time
the queen of the night
comes into full flower

oh, the fleeting life
of this flower—
from amongst its leaves
a queen of the night *unfolds*
lushly into full bloom

it's as if they are breathing…
while I watch
the buds
on the queen of the night
are swelling, opening

I watched
the single-minded efforts
of this flower to bloom,
unaware
of holding my breath

Destiny

束の間の
命を咲くと
月下美人
まもりて心
おごそかにあり

清き香を
頼りて行けば
白々と
夜目にもしるき
月下美人の花

折あらば
又会ひたしと
思ひるし
人なり訃報
読みつつ悔し　　　　（訃報）

10

when this queen of the night
blooms into
its brief life,
I'm guarding it
with solemn heart

when I go there
following its pure fragrance,
the queen of the night
is visible, white and clear
in the darkness

if only there had been time
to see her once again
I thought,
reading the obituary
with deep regret   (Obituary)

廃屋

<ruby>獄<rt>ひとや</rt></ruby> にて
あるかも知れず
石の廃屋
高窓一つ
閉ざされしまま

<ruby>繋<rt>つな</rt></ruby>がれるし
人の思ひを
計りつつ
見上ぐる窓の
厚く小さく

The Deserted House

it may have been

a prison, perhaps—

the single high window

of the deserted stone house

stays tightly shut

conjecturing

about a prisoner

held in chains here,

I gaze up

at the small, thick, window

五人の子

五人の子
それぞれ直<ruby>直<rt>なほ</rt></ruby>く
世にあれば
独り居りつつ
心足らひぬ

誇るには
あらねど心
満ち足りぬ
五人の子皆
直く世に生き

憂ひごと
多かりしよと
五人の子
人と成りたる
今にして思ふ

子を持てば
おのづからにし
親さびて
ふるまひるるも
我が子ら五人

14

Five Children

with five children

respectively

in their right places

in the world, I am

well content to be alone

though it is not

a matter for pride,

I feel satisfied

all my five children

live well in this world

many worries

came with a family

of five children,

I think now

looking back on it

having children

themselves, now

my five children

of their own accord

are acting like parents

一つの悔

若き日は
ひたすら子らに
かかはりゐて
老母見る日の
稀なりし悔

我が齢
老いづき初めし
昨日今日
亡き母のこと
頻り思はる

はぐれたる
母を探せる
夢なりき
覚めても暫し
心悲しく

潔斎と
いふにはあらね
浄めたる
机の上に
師の歌書を開く

16

One Regret

in my younger days
so entirely involved
with my children,
I rarely saw my aged mother —
how I regret that now

beginning
to get old myself,
yesterday
and today I think
often of my deceased mother

I dreamed of searching
for my lost mother —
when I awoke
my heart ached
for quite a while

not exactly
ritual purification, but
I clean my desk
before opening on it
the teacher's book of poems

朝夕

大屯山に
<ruby>大屯山<rt>だいとんざん</rt></ruby>に
ま向ひ住みて
幾年ぞ
登り見ん日を
思ひ続けつつ

暁の
散歩の道に
行きあひし
農婦の籠の
<ruby>茄子<rt>なす</rt></ruby>の紫

幾年も
待ちし山茶花の
初蕾
葉を分けにつつ
数確かめぬ

送られし
山茶花の実
地に埋めて
待ちしかひあり
蕾持ちたり

18

Morning and Evening

living directly opposite
Mt. Daiton
for a number of years
I continue to contemplate
the day I will climb it

the purple color
of eggplants in the basket
of a farmer's wife
I met as I set out
to walk the dawn path

after a wait of some years,
the sasanqua
has its first buds —
parting the leaves, I
checked how many buds

I buried in the earth
the sasanqua seeds
sent to me —
my wait was worthwhile
when the buds came forth

紫の
拘杞の小花よ
拘杞よしと
勧めし人も
逝きて年経ぬ

この朝け
露台に立てば
遠寺の
経読む声の
風に乗り来る

久しくも
聞かざるままに
忘れるし
山鳩の声
今朝の寝覚めに

鈴生りの
下枝の蜜柑
自が重みに
耐へかねて皆
土に坐りぬ

oh, the tiny purple flowers
on the kuko shrub —
the person who
recommended kuko to me
passed away, years ago

today at dawn
when I stand on the balcony,
a voice reading the sutra
in the distant temple
is borne to me on the breeze

forgotten, as though
unheard for a long, long, time
the voice
of a turtledove
as I wake this morning

laden with mandarins
the lower branches
can't bear their weight
and they are all
sitting on the ground

咲き盛る
菊に混りて
ダリアの花
咲き初めて形
日々に整ふ

冬づきて
温泉町の
道のべに
立つ湯烟は
暖かく見ゆ

若き日

気負ひつつ
世に 逆 ひし
　　さから
若き日の
我を親はも
憂ひたるらし

いつしかに
声尖りつつ
物言ひるる
我にてありしと
ふと言葉切る

mingled with the abundance
of chrysanthemums
are dahlias blooming
for the first time, day by day
becoming well-shaped

winter has come:
on the roadsides
of this hot-spring town
the steam welling up
looks so warm

My Young Days

my young days
when eagerly I
swam against the stream —
how anxious my parents
must have been

when I realize
I've unconsciously
raised my voice
while talking,
I suddenly break off

我らが運命

国連の投票により台湾の地位決めらるといふ

審判を
待つ身の心地
この日頃
心集めて
ニュース読むわれ

我が安危
国際与論の
手にありと
おのが運命を
しみじみ思ふ

これよりの
道は厳しと
初老わが
覚悟をわれと
われに言ひ聞かす

大方の
世を生きて来て
今はただ
心からなる
安らぎを思ふ

24

Our Destiny

The United Nations' vote will determine the status of Taiwan, we're told.

my feelings
as I await the judgment…
these days
I read the news
with bated breath

with my safety
lying in the hands of
international public opinion,
I feel keenly
this sense of destiny

the road ahead
will be tough,
I tell myself
as I enter old age
to be prepared

having lived
the majority of my life
now, it is
only a matter, I feel,
of resting whole-heartedly

たはやすく
真実言はぬは
生きてゆく
一つの知恵と
思ひ知らさる

台湾の
題字に続き
国連追放とふ
字に堪へて居り
ニュース読みつつ

大勢[たいせい]に
あらがふ術[すべ]なし
今はただ
流れのままに
身を委[ゆだ]ねなん

父母の
いづれにつくかと
迫られし
子のまどひにも
似るこの心

that one cannot tell the truth
without constraint,
is a piece of wisdom
which becomes evident
as one goes through life

'Taiwan'
following the headlines
I bear up
while reading of its expulsion
by the United Nations

there is no way
we can oppose the current situation,
so now it's simply
a matter of entrusting ourselves
to the flow of events

which of my parents
do I cleave to?
in this heart of mine
the dilemma of a child
driven to the last ditch

おのがじし
思ひ余りて
隣人ら
寄れば声をぞ
ひそめ物言ふ

おのが国
語る声遂に
怒り帯び
嗚咽<ruby>鳴咽<rt>をえつ</rt></ruby>となりぬ
ベトナムの友

<ruby>何方<rt>いづかた</rt></ruby>に
向くべき怒りか
ベトナムの
友の訴へ
かりそめならず

not knowing what to do
about their individual concerns,
the neighbors
get together
and talk in whispers

the voice
of my Vietnamese friend
as she speaks of her country
eventually breaks down
into furious sobbing

where should her anger
be directed?
the complaints
of my Vietnamese friend
won't simply go away

Destiny

1972

友情

歌誌潮音の誌上に於て東京府立一高女時代の旧友と連絡つく

国変り
時過ぎ断たれしと
思ひるし
友情帰る
潮音歌誌に

朝空を
行く鳩群の
白き腹
羽搏く毎に
光りつ翳りつ

冬の陽を
一葉一葉に
受けとめて
椿燦然
まなかひに立つ

菜を担ぎ
朝市に急ぐ
母の背に
児はまろまろと
目を開けてをり

Friendship

Contact with an old friend from the Tokyo Prefectural First Girls' High School, in the pages of the *tanka* magazine, *Chō-On.*

after changing countries

and the passage of time,

I thought it severed

but our friendship came back

on the pages of Chō-On

white-bellied, a flock of doves

rises into the morning sky,

wings flapping

each in turn

shining and shadowing

every leaf

catching the winter sun

the camellia bush

stands radiant

before my eyes

hurrying to morning market

with her burden

of greens,

the mother carries on her back

an infant with round open eyes

老いづく

口にこそ
言はね幾つか
不調_{ふてうかしよ}個処
身に持ちてなほ
老に耐へんとす

老いづきて
目のたるみまで
母に似ると
つくづく見入る
我が朝鏡

長き夜を
寝足らひ覚めて
床の中に
作らん歌を
想ふひと時

幼孫らアメリカより帰省、ベビーシッターを勤めて孫らと共に遊ぶ

乳首_{ちくび}含み
目閉ぢて寝よと
老われを
ベビーに仕立てぬ
幼き孫ら

Old Age Arrives

bearing with me
a number of troubles
which I don't voice,
I will endeavor
to endure as I age

now old age is here
I resemble my mother —
looking carefully
in the morning mirror, I see
even the same bags under my eyes

waking after a long night
of sufficient sleep
I've time, in bed,
to imagine the tanka
I might write

My young grandchildren return home. I act as baby-sitter and play with them.

suck on the nipple,
close your eyes, and go to sleep
says my young grandchild
wanting to make this old me
into a baby

抱ける児の
落しし玩具
拾ひつつ
祖母も体力
要（い）るものと思ふ

露満ちし
グリーンにボールの
描きたる
ゆるき弧の跡
朝目にしむる　　　　　　　（新淡水ゴルフリンク）

僅かなる
水に伸び行く
水仙の
芽よと見る間に
蕾顕ち来ぬ

picking up the toy
dropped by the child
held in my arms
this grandma, too, I think
needs plenty of strength

on the dew-laden green
traces of the gentle curve
described by a ball
linger shimmering
in my eyes this morning   (New Tamsui Golf Links)

barely had I seen
the sprouts of narcissus
that had grown
with little watering,
than buds appeared there

この 朝^{あした}
身うちに力
溢れ来て
生きゐる幸を
しみじみ思ふ

温泉の
湯壺の中に
沈みゐて
知れる限りの
唱歌うたひ見ぬ

ひと時の
安らぎを手に
抱くごと
温泉の中に
独り沈みをり

38

this morning
I am overflowing
with energy,
feeling keenly the good fortune
of being alive

immersing myself
in the hot spring spa
I tried singing
as many as I remembered
of the songs taught at school

as if embracing
a time of relaxation
I immerse myself
alone in the waters
of the hot spring

廃坑の町

亡き父の
心砕きし
炭山は
荒れたるままに
人影もなし

黒ダイヤと
言ひて掘りたる
人ら何処
残れるボタに
小雨そぼ降る

ここに生^あれ
ここに死ぬるか
廃坑の
町に老らは
細々と生く

The Abandoned Mine Town

the coal mine
that my deceased father
took great pains
to keep going, now in ruins
with no vestiges of people

where are the people
who called what they excavated
'black diamonds'?
on the remaining slag-heap
a light rain falls

born here
will they die here?
in the abandoned mine town
the elderly spending
their narrow lives

地に籠りし兵

赤き心を
点（とも）して兵は
地の底に
細々生きゐし
二十八年　　　　　　　　　　　（横井庄一氏グアム島に発見さる）

横井氏の
律義な言葉
遠き世の
事に思ひつつ
詳（つぶさ）に読みぬ

地にひそみ
兵の精神
貫きし
二十八年
孤独の月日

一筋の
赤心（せきしん）持ちて
地に籠り
二十八年
ながらへし兵

42

The Soldier Holed Up In The Ground

the soldier
with a shining red heart,
underground
barely getting by
for twenty-eight years   (Yokoi Shōichi is discovered on Guam)

while considering
Mr. Yokoi's sincere account
as something
from a distant world,
I read it with close attention

lurking in the earth
drilled in the martial spirit
twenty-eight years
of solitary days
and months

with straight and true heart,
holed up in the ground
for twenty-eight years
he lived on
as a soldier

障子張り

孫どもの
置き土産なる
障子穴
老の腰据ゑ
幾日繕ふ

障子穴
傑作主の
児の面輪<ruby>面輪<rt>おもわ</rt></ruby>
思ひ出でつつ
手繕ひをり

May Yen Ting

Papering the *Shōji*

souvenirs of my grandchildren,
these holes they've made
in the shōji *screens*
squatting my old body
I take some days for the repairs

mentally picturing
the face of that child
who is master
of making the holes,
I'm repairing the screens

迫り来るもの

千余字の
コミュニケに
我が運命は
定められぬと
厳かに読む　　　　　　　（ニクソン氏大陸に行く）

転々と
歴史の波に
揺られては
渡され行く島
我が生れし島

刻々と
迫り来るもの
身に覚え
如何になるらん
明日かと思ふ

May Yen Ting

A Threat Hanging Over Me

in a communiqué
of a thousand words or more
my fate
has been determined,
I read solemnly   (Mr. Nixon goes to the mainland)

rolled this way and that
by the waves of history,
the island
where I was born
is being handed over

minute by minute
conscious of the threat
hanging over me,
I wonder what
tomorrow will bring

春色

気兼ねなく
空家の庭に
伸びさせし
桜の枝は
今花盛り

身を抱き
頭振るごと
<ruby>相思樹<rt>さうしじゆ</rt></ruby>は
あるとも見えぬ
風に揺れゐる

中天に
抜き立つ椰子の
木立まで
あかあか染めて
陽は入らんとす

Spring Colors

the branches of cherry trees
growing unrestrained
in the garden
of an empty house,
are laden now with blooms

there's the acacia
looking like it's holding itself
and shaking its head
while it sways in a breeze
invisible to me

as the sun sinks
it dyes vivid red
the stand
of palm trees thrusting
high into the sky

「頭後屈」
高圧線に
鳥がゐて
我が体操を
見下してゐる

寝屋近き
ユーカリに鳴く
鳥の音に
いつも目覚むる
習ひとなりぬ

数々の
鳥の音に朝
目覚むるも
幸の一つと
思ふこの頃

on the high voltage wire
there are birds
gazing down
at me while
I do my exercises

I've got into the habit
of always opening my eyes
when I hear
birds chirping in the eucalypt
near my bedroom

waking each morning
to the sounds from many birds,
is one of my blessings
I have been feeling
recently

Destiny

並木路の
若葉トンネル
行く人の
影も緑に
染まるこのごろ

川上に
工事場あるか
薬罐提げて
人らは朝の
流れに沿ひ行く

工夫提げる
薬罐の反射
次々に
朝の田の面を
眩く照らす

the shadows of people
walking through the tunnel
formed by an avenue
of trees with young leaves,
are colored green, these days

on the river's upper reaches
is there perhaps a work site?
thermos flasks in hand
people are walking
along its bank, this morning

dazzling glimmers
on the surface of the morning paddies
from reflections
of a succession of thermos flasks
carried along by the workers

母の声

山荘の
子を呼び戻す
母の声
血を吐く思ひ
籠りてやゐん　　　　　　　（浅間山荘に赤軍籠る）

むざむざと
若きら命
奪はれて
この世に生きて
行く厳しさ思ふ　　　　　（富士山の雪崩に青年数多死ぬ）

アポロ16号

月面<ruby>げつめん</ruby>に
今人ありと
思ひ見る
弦月椰子の
上にさやけし

活動の
飛行士何処
月面の
クレーターに
暫し 眸<ruby>ひとみ</ruby>をこらす

The Mother's Voice

at the mountain villa
calling her child home
the voice of the mother
must be filled with
desperate urgency　　　　　　(the Red Army holed up at Asama Mountain Villa)

how easily
those young ones
were robbed of their lives—
I reflect on the harshness
of dwelling in this world　　　　(many youths killed in an avalanche on Mt. Fuji)

Apollo 16

there are now people
on the moon's surface
I think, gazing at
the crescent moon shining
brightly over the palm trees

for a while
I fix my gaze on the crater
of the moon's surface
trying to see where
astronauts are active

散歩に通ふ丘

ゆくりなく
村落に来て
聞く薪割りの
響かふ音に
心なごむも

犬二匹
孫の童女と
人形と
連れたる老爺
朝の散策

すぼめたる
傘の形に
野の朝顔
露立つ朝を
まだ眠りをり

向ひるる
山の緑に
思ひきり
口中見せし
起きがけのあくび

Walking Up a Hill

coming by chance
to a small village
I hear the echoing
sound of wood-chopping,
a sound to soothe my heart

the old man's morning ramble
taking along
two dogs, and
a little granddaughter
plus her doll

in the shape
of folded umbrellas
wild morning-glories
still sleeping away
this misty morning

arising, I give
a great yawn
opening wide my mouth
towards the green
of the mountain opposite

丘に佇ちて
野山の緑
鳥の音を
皆我が物と
思ふひと時

切りぎしに
早朝の 行
する男
坐せる 巖 の
一つとなりゐる

クラス会
もとの才女も
孫と嫁と
神経痛に
話落ちつく

standing on the hill
I feel, at this moment,
as if the greenery
of fields and mountain
and birdsong, are all mine

in early morning —
on the steep cliff
a man sitting
in ascetic practice
turns into a rock

at our class reunion
the woman who was our 'genius'
settled to chat
about neuralgia and
her grandsons and daughters-in-law

折にふれて

二年寝て
逝きたる母に
我が姿
重ね見てより
一つのこの危惧

馬鹿正直と
人は言へども
おのづから
又得るものの
ある世と思ふ

Occasionally

my one fear

is seeing myself become

like my mother,

bed-ridden for two years

then passing away

though people say

I am honest to a fault,

my belief is that

in this world there may be something

to be gained by being honest

師にまみゆ

一九七二年五月二十四日植松節子操、森友とし子様と共に鎌倉の四賀光子師を訪ぬ

師の許に
急ぐ車中の
友三人
語らひ弾みて
弾み放しに

命ありて
五十年今日
師の君に
まみゆる我ぞ
夫も連れだち

迷へる子
戻り来し如く
師の胸に
よよと泣きたし
五十年の事

May Yen Ting

Meeting My Teacher

On May 24, 1972, together with Uematsu Setsuko-sama and Moritomo Toshiko-sama, I visited our teacher, Shiga Mitsuko-sensei.

we hastened

to our teacher's house,

three friends

in a car chatting,

spurred on, letting go

today

fifty years of life later

I'm meeting you,

dear teacher, this time

accompanied by my husband

like a child

who has strayed and

returned to the fold

fifty years later, I want

to sob in my teacher's arms

Destiny

慈母にそふ
如く貴き
もの抱く
ごとく師とありて
一日の幸

五月晴（さつきばれ）
指さす山荘
杳々と（よう）
緑の中に
埋もりてをり（うづ）　　　　　　　　（師の御住居杳々山荘といふ）

東京府立第一高女の先輩井戸川美和子様を待つ

五十年
見ぬ友を待てば
デートする
をとめの如く
胸高鳴るも

like a beloved mother
like somebody precious
this teacher
I embrace on a day
of good fortune

this fine day in May
the teacher's mountain house
we point to
is dimly visible
buried in greenery   (our teacher's dwelling is called Yō-Yō Villa)

Waiting for Idogawa Miwako-sama, a senior student when I was at the Tokyo Prefectural First Girls' High School.

as I wait
for a friend not seen
in fifty years
my heart is singing
like a young girl on a date

子らを訪ねて渡米

太平洋
越え来て子らに
先づ言ふは
手紙に書けぬ
故国の事ども 　　　　　　（五月二十五日）

久に会ふ
子の成長は
嬉しけれど
いつか労はられるる
わが老佗し

客ながら
縫ひ繕ひに
草取りに
次々して来ぬ
どの子の家にも

Going to America to Visit My Children

having crossed the Pacific Ocean
the first thing I talk about
to the children
is the old country's issues,
which I can't write in letters   (May 25)

though I delight
in the growth of the child
not met in a long while,
when treated with care
I pity myself for being old

although a guest
in all of my children's homes
I end up
doing the mending, weeding gardens,
one task after another

ワシントン

ブラックパワー
濶歩するは皆
ニグロなり
首都ワシントン
日曜の町

エレベーター
ニグロ人らの
中にゐて
昇る間を
息潜め居し

昼暗き
エレベーターと
目凝らせば
ニグロら張りつく
如く立ちをり

Washington

Black Power —
all blacks, they are
striding out
in the Sunday streets
of Washington the capital

standing in the elevator
amongst a crowd
of blacks,
I was holding my breath
as we ascended

in the daytime
peering into the dark elevator
I see
blacks standing there
as if stuck on the spot

ニューヨーク

ニューヨーク
雑多人種の
列にゐて
せかせかと追ふ
辻の緑燈

全人種
コンベヤにある
如く行く
タイムズスクエア
休日の宵

ザ・ステーツ
黒・白・褐色・
黄色人を
徐々ミクスし行く
人種の坩堝　　　　　　　　（合衆国）

老華僑
雑沓の町の
家の門に
腰掛けて読みゐるは
故国の便りか

New York

walking in a line
of New York's
multi-cultural folk,
I rush to obey the green light
at each street corner

it's as if
all the peoples of the world
are on a conveyor belt,
when I walk through Times Square
the evening of a public holiday

the States
is a crucible
with its gradual mixing
of races—black, white,
brown and yellow   (The United States)

an old Chinese immigrant
sits at the gate of a house
in the busy town,
reading a letter—maybe
it's from his country of birth

このままに
異国に朽ちるか
チャイナタウンを
よろめきい行く
襤褸の　翁
<ruby>襤<rt>らん</rt>褸<rt>る</rt></ruby>の　<ruby>翁<rt>おきな</rt></ruby>

ただ独り
絨毯を踏む音
いや冴えて
ホテルの長廊
坑道の如し　　　　　　　　（アストリアホテル）

ホテル出でて
開放感に
ふと掛けし
公園のベンチ
去り難くゐる　　　　　　　（セントラルパーク）

リスと豆
分け合ひにつつ
若きらの
語らひ眺むる
公園のベンチ

72

will he
wither away like this
in an alien land?
an old man in rags
staggers through Chinatown

so clear, the sound
of my solitary footsteps
on the carpet—
this long hotel corridor
feels like the tunnel of a mine   (Hotel Astoria)

when I get out of the hotel
there's a sense of liberation,
then it's hard to leave
the park bench
I sat on by chance   (Central Park)

sharing peanuts
with the squirrels
as I sit
on the park bench, I watch
the young ones chattering

チャイナタウン・
ハレームのごみ・
落書に
汚れしままの
大ニューヨーク

けたたまし
救急車行く
頻度にも
大を示すか
ニューヨークの町

我が運を
ためす心地に
空飛ぶや
相次ぐ事故の
記事読みながら　　　　　　　　（日航機・泰国機連続の遭難）

74

the rubbish
of Chinatown
and Harlem
and this great New York
desecrated with graffiti

is the greatness
of New York city
demonstrated
by the frequency of
ambulances screaming past?

in the spirit
of testing my luck,
I fly through the sky
while reading articles
about a succession of accidents (the series of misfortunes for Japan Airlines and Thai Air)

スペインところどころ

迷宮に
入りし思ひに
王最期の
室へと暗き
廊幾曲り　　　　　　　　（七月五日より欧洲に渡る）

王朝の
栄華を留めて
地下墓所に
光る二十六
大理石棺

勇士眠る
巌窟の上の
十字架を
ただ目じるしの
スペイン枯野

Places Here and There in Spain

thinking I've wandered

into a labyrinth,

I make several turns

around dark corridors

to get to the King's death chamber   (traveling to Europe on July 5)

with the glory

of the dynasty at an end,

twenty-six marble coffins

lie gleaming

in an underground mausoleum

the grottos

where heroes sleep

marked only

with a cross,

on the dry Spanish plain

不毛地に
咲かせし人間の
技の華
トレード丘野
石の殿堂

May I ask you を
連発しつつ
国々の
町を旅行く
初老の二人

in this barren land
the magnificence
of man's arts and crafts
flowers in the stone pantheons
of the Toledo hills

with a volley
of 'May I ask you'
questions, two oldies
travel around towns
in various countries

パリの町

フランスの
革命広場
コンコルドに
悲しく聞きぬ
アントワネットの名

王朝の
罪身に負ひて
立たされし
広場の台か
マリアアントワネット

貴族に生れ
華やかに生き
痛ましく
逝きぬと仰ぐ
画姿優し

May Yen Ting

The City of Paris

in the Place de la Concorde,
the site of the French revolution,
I heard
with such sadness
that name Marie Antoinette

this platform in the square—
is it the very one on which
Marie Antoinette stood
shouldering the crimes
of the French dynasty?

born into the nobility
she led a glamorous life
but died a painful death,
I think looking up
at the picture of her gentle figure

左見右見
ナポレオンの名
負ふ棺ぞ
寺院ま中に
赤大理石

遠近の
跡皆息づきて
国々の
人を招きゐる
夏のパリの町

looking around
I found a coffin
bearing the name Napoleon
in the very center of the temple —
it was made of red marble

far and near
each of the monuments
seems to be alive, and
inviting people from all over
to summer in Paris

ロンドン

ロンドン塔
恨みの霊か
巡りるて
王冠の列
妖(あや)しく光る

沙翁(さをう)像
ポーズせる手に
どこよりか
鳩飛び来ては乗る
スクエアの朝

Hi(ハイ) と寄りて
声を掛けたし
ニュートンの
像は路傍(ろばう)に
ありて小さし

London

at the Tower of London
are they malicious ghosts
wandering around?
I see rows of crowns
gleaming eerily

morning in the square:
from somewhere or other
pigeons keep flying in
to rest on the outstretched hand
of the statue of Shakespeare

'Hi' I wanted to say,
approaching the statue
of Newton
by the roadside,
such a small statue

ヘンリー王の

五夫人妍を

競ひし日や

棚に残れる

綺羅も色褪せ

ザ・グレートブリテン　　（大英帝国）

町を行く

タクシー

細い銭まで

皆重々し

King Henry's five wives
those times of rivaling beauties —
on some shelves
remain their gorgeous garments,
colors all faded

Great Britain:
the taxis going along
through this town
are all so ponderous
even to their small change

オランダ

コスチュームに
木靴も軽く
乙女らが
運河縫ひ行く
マルケン漁村

牛羊
思ひ思ひに
<ruby>屯<rt>たむろ</rt></ruby>して
オランダ低地
緑果てなし

シンボルに
今は立ちゐる
風車
廻れるもあり
廻らぬもあり

88

May Yen Ting

Holland

at Marken fishing village
young girls in costume
with wooden clogs
treading lightly, as they
weave their way along the canals

the greenness
of Holland's lowlands
seems to stretch forever,
with cattle and sheep
camped here and there

these symbols
of Holland, the windmills
still standing now:
some of them turn
some of them don't turn

ベルギー

レース綴る
老婆の手許
確かにて
しかも手早し
ブラッセル土産物店

小便小僧
はにかみてや居ん
建物の
陰に小さく
像立ちてをり

ウォーターロー
麦畑中に
築きたる
碑に語らする
激戦の跡

Belgium

at a souvenir shop
in Brussels,
an old woman
tatting lace, working
with precision and speed

standing
in the shadow of a building
the small statue,
'Manneken Pis'—
he must be shy

that monument
erected in the middle
of a Waterloo wheat field
speaks of the aftermath
of fierce fighting

風切りつ
羽搏きつして
太公国
古城を巡る
夏つばくらめ　　　　　　　（ルクセンブルグ）

太公国
丘の緑を
占めゐるは
米兵の墓
十字架の列　　　　　　　（第二次世界大戦々跡）

beating against the wind,
flapping their wings,
summer swallows
fly around the old castle
of the monarchy   (Luxembourg)

occupying green space
on the hill of this monarchy
are rows of crosses
which mark the graves
of American soldiers   (traces of World War II)

スイス

スロープの
緑に牛も
浸^{ひた}りるる
悠久平和の
山国スイス

遠近^{をちこち}に
吊られし
白き干し物も
景を添へるる
スイスの緑野

青巒^{せいらん}の
縁^{ふち}どるスイス
スロープに
白壁の家あり
黄牛群れて

May Yen Ting

Switzerland

the cattle seem immersed
in the greenery on the slopes
of this country
of permanent peace,
Switzerland

part of the scenery
in these green fields
of Switzerland
is the washing hanging
whitely, near and far

on the slopes
of the blue peaks
rimming Switzerland
are white-walled houses
and herds of yellow cows

アルプスの
<ruby>落水<rt>らくする</rt></ruby>スイスの
飲み水は
夏も冷たき
透明ミルク

アルプスの
斜面の緑を
ま二つに
<ruby>截<rt>た</rt></ruby>ちて落水
<ruby>一条<rt>ひとすぢ</rt></ruby>白く

the run-off
from alpine streams
is Swiss drinking water,
cool even in summer
as is their translucent milk

dividing the green slope
of an alpine mountain
exactly in two
is a white ribbon
of falling water

ドイツ

兵列に
立てし葡萄の
支へに見る
国民性よ
ライン峡谷 　　　　　　（ライン河を溯る）

植ゑ植ゑて
天に至るか
ライン峡谷
急な傾斜も
皆葡萄園

菜の青に
紛れず咲ける
罌粟一つ
赤くぞ見ゆる
ラインの河原

髪を梳く
乙女の岩に聞く
ローレライ
馴染みの歌よ
胸熱くなる

Germany

the nature of the people
seems like what I see
in the Rhine Valley:
grape-growing in martial rows
with fixed supports   *(traveling up the Rhine)*

plants and more plants,
will they reach the sky?
the steep slopes
of this Rhine Valley
are all covered with vineyards

separate from the green
of the mustard plants,
one single poppy
blooms red—I glimpse it
on the bank of the Rhine

hearing the familiar song
of the Lorelei, on the rock
where a maiden
combs her hair,
I'm warmed with pleasure

乙女ありし
所か今は
旗立ちて
楽のメロデイに
揺れゐるる如し

畑毎の
実り程度を
だんだらの
模様に見せる
バヴアリア麦野

遠き代の
王を身近かに
覚えたり
遺愛の肘掛け
脂_{あぶらあか}垢の痕_{あと}　　　　　（バヴアリアの古き王城）

is this the place
where the maiden was?
now a flag stands
fluttering there,
as if playing that melody

the degree of ripeness
in each field, shows
in parallel-striped patterns
on the wheat plains
of Bavaria

I felt a sense
of nearness to the kings
of distant ages —
on the cherished elbow rests,
marks of grease and grime   *(the old Bavarian Royal Palace)*

第二次世界大戦の時、ダッハウにユダヤ人の集中営ありてここに大虐殺行はれたり

二十万
ユダヤの鬼哭も
啾々と
混りて渡るか
ダッハウ麦野の風

目をやりつ
そらしつ見行く
キャンパスの
ユダヤ人ありし
日の実写真

運び来し
ビール旨けれど
ポツダムホテル
従業員の
表情なき顔

During World War II, Jewish people were rounded up and sent to the concentration camp at Dachau, where most of them were killed.

are wails and cries

from the spirits

of 200,000 Jews

mingled with the wind blowing

across the Dachau wheat fields?

I walk around

gazing here, averting my gaze there—

actual photographs

of the days when Jews

occupied this camp

the beer he brought

is delicious—but

there is no expression

on the face of the waiter

at the Potsdam hotel

オーストリア

山紫水明
偽りならず
尖塔の
寺囲みゐる
チロルの村々

悠々と
葡萄畑の
野を分けて
古城の下を
巡るドナウ河

ドナウ河はウイーンを過ぎてチエツコスロバキア・ハンガリー・ユーゴースラビア・
ブルガリア・ルーマニア・ソ連等共産国を流れて黒海に入る

ドナウ河
謳はれしブルーの
色見せず
これより赤き
国へ入り行く

Austria

this scenic beauty

is no lie:

Tyrolean villages

surrounded by churches

with pointed steeples

winding below

the old castles

dividing

vast fields of grapevines,

is the river Danube

Once past Vienna, the Danube flows through Communist countries such as Czechoslovakia, Hungary, Yugoslavia, Bulgaria, Romania, and countries of the Soviet Union, before emptying into the Black Sea.

I cannot see

the blue of the 'Blue Danube'

they sing about—

next we will be going

into red countries

舗道行く
馬車の蹄の
音冴えて
ウィーンの古都に
ひと日始まる

露天店
コーヒー一杯に
衢見て
時忘れゐる
ヨーロッパの人

終日の
Tour bus にて
音もせぬ
文字のままなる
ゼントルメンら

a day in the old city
of Vienna
begins with the clear sound
of clip-clopping horse carts
along the cobbled ways

sitting in open-air cafés,
with cups of coffee
beside them, Europeans
watch the street life
and forget about time

on the full day
tour bus,
quiet as mice,
the gentlemen behave
like gentlemen

野菜など
何処こ植うる
ヨーロッパの
丘も野も皆
葡萄園のみ

弱き歯に
そろり嚙みるし
堅パンの
味覚え来て
旅終らんとす

ハイジャックの
間接被害か
エアポートに
老幼残らず
身体捜査

where do they grow
vegetables and so on?
these European hills and dales
completely covered
just with vineyards

I have come to know
the taste of that hard bread
I've chewed so slowly
with my weak teeth —
now that this trip is ending

is this the aftermath
of hijacking incidents?
at the airport, each person
old and young alike
is subjected to a body search

ブダの国タイ

地球一周の
旅 恙^{つつが}なく
タイに入り
蓮華^{れんげ}捧げて
ブダ拝みたり

メナム河の
うねり行く野に
聳えたる
パゴダ形も
色もとりどり

釈迦牟尼の
一生刻みて
十七年
一枚板の
細工精細^{せいさい}　　　　　　　（バンコツク博物館）

110

Thailand, Country of the Buddha

our round-the-world trip
going without a hitch
we enter Thailand,
then carrying lotus flowers
make obeisance to the Buddha

from the fields
beside the winding Menam River,
pagodas
soar into the sky
all shapes and colors

the life
of Gautama Buddha:
seventeen years
of carving with delicate workmanship
onto a single piece of wood   *(Bangkok Museum)*

跪_{ひざまづ}き
黄金_{わうごん}のブダ
拝みるる
タイの人らの
黒き足裏_{あなうら}

極彩色
寺の重ねし
屋根の尖
そりゐて舞の
五指にぞ似たる

タイ故宮の
亭_{ちん}の敷石に
男らは
四肢投げ出して
夏日の午睡

the black soles
of Thai people
kneeling
to worship
a golden Buddha

roof-tops of multiple
brightly colored temples
pointing up and bending back
resemble the five fingers
of Thai dancers

on paving stones
in front of the pavilions
of the ancient palace
men are sprawled out
taking a siesta, this summer day

一つの憂ひ

朋月や
訴へて詮なし
千余万の
胸を占めるる
一つの憂ひ

我等孤舟^{こしう}
にある心地して
西東
向くも歴史の
波寄するまま

秋逝く日
切り捨てられし
小国の
民の悲哀を
胸に秘めをり

我ら同胞
イズムはおきて
父母の
和成る日を今は
ひたすら思ふ

A Single Source of Grief

ah, bright moon,
useless to complain—
a single source of grief
is occupying
more than a million hearts

we feel as though
we're in a lone boat—
facing west or east
we find ourselves at the mercy
of the waves of history

the sorrow of the people
in this small country
abandoned
at the end of autumn
is concealed in our hearts

setting aside
the doctrine of our countrymen,
I pray earnestly
for the day the father and mother
will make peace

血を分けし
同胞なれば
いつの日か
一つになると
人ら肯^{うべな}ふ

心ならずも
置きて来し父母
妻子あり
大陸よ目に見えて
その道遠し

国の危期
救ひし功は
攫^{さら}はれて
老雄島に
悲願持ちてをり

かりそめの
今の寧^{やす}さよ
積みためし
歌書をひたすら
読み急ぐなり

separate blood
and the same placenta —
will there come a day
when we people
consent to unify?

involuntarily
father, mother, wife or children
have been left behind
on the mainland —
though visible it's so distant

that merit which saved the country
in its time of peril
now snatched from him,
the old hero stays on the island
holding to his long-cherished desire

in the temporary peace
of the here and now,
I hasten to read
seriously, those tanka *collections*
which have been piling up

秋日

湧き上がる
湯元の烟
ちぎれては
散りつつ空の
青になり行く

朝毎の
体操に立つ
丘の上
一株咲ける
赤まんまの側

南国の
秋を自負する
如くにも
穂芒白く
万緑に顕つ

韋駄天に
我を抜き行ける
若きらの
背にゆらゆら
秋陽添ひ行く

118

Autumn Days

the smoke
billowing up
from the hot springs
scatters here, scatters there,
as it joins the blue of the sky

beside me on the hill-top
where I stand every morning
doing my exercises,
a bush of inutade *weed*
is in bloom now

as if conceited
about this southern land's autumn,
the pampas ears
stand white
amongst a myriad greens

autumn sunlight
is wavering on the backs
of the young people
as they go past me
like swift runners

或る帰国

浦島に
ならで帰りし
岡田女史
我も名知れば
胸を撫でをり　　　　　　　（岡田嘉子）

一場の
長かりし劇よ
国境越えの
ヒロイン帰りて
幕となりけり

癌病む友

術<ruby>すべ</ruby>尽きし
癌症を
友語るなり
秋の夕日に
眼<ruby>まなこ</ruby> 向けつつ

われ忌み言ふ
癌を淡々と
言ひ出でし
友に向ひて
心救はる

120

A Certain Homecoming

the homecoming
of Ms. Okada was not
like Urashima Tarō's —
knowing the full story,
I felt relieved   (Okada Yoshiko)

it was a play
with one long act:
the curtain fell on its heroine
crossing national borders
to return home

My Friend Suffering from Cancer

out of treatment options
my friend talks
about her cancer symptoms,
eyeballing me
in the evening sun of autumn

for me, 'cancer'
is a taboo topic,
yet facing my friend
as she spoke calmly of it,
relieved my mind

亡き母

老いづきし
同胞_{はらから}寄れば
父に似し
母に似し顔
各々並ぶ

あの世より
汝ら_{なれ}守らんと
母言ひき
恃むともなく
恃みるるらし

幾月の
昏睡覚めて
母は先づ
命拾ひしと
しみじみ言ひぬ

失語せし
母まじまじと
我らを見て
疾く逝かせよと_と
手振りに言ふも

122

My Deceased Mother

now that old age has hit them,
in the faces of my siblings
when they are together
I see this one is like our father,
that one resembles our mother

my mother told me
to protect you
from the outside world—
without realizing, it seems
we're dependent on her words

coming out of a coma
after several months,
first of all
my mother spoke movingly
of having a narrow escape

at a loss for words,
my mother
stared at us
gesturing as if to say
'let me die quickly'

恐惶

人の世の
絶体絶命
かくや唯
声を限りに
家人の名を喚ぶ

無事に又
今日を迎へし
幸ひを
しかと抱きて
朝床にをり

逝く年に
攫はれたるか
友・知己の
訃報次々
来て我を襲ふ

誰彼の
訃報相次ぐ
昨日今日
近火に独り
身のある心地

Fearful and Unsettled

so this is
the last extremity
of the human world—
I call out my family's names
with what voice I have left

in bed in the morning
I firmly embrace
the good fortune
of having arrived safely
at another day

at the end of the year
I am overwhelmed by
a succession of death notices
of friends and acquaintances
who've been carried off

one another come
the death notices
of this one and that—
today I feel the flames
licking at my solitary self

神仏も
祈らず悟りも
なきままに
老い来て今日を
一つの惑ひ

袂より
無産者新聞を
そと呉れし
友よ年経て
名も 朧 ^{おぼろ}なり

千九百
七十二年の
多事多端に
堪へ来て命
いよよ愛^{いと}しも

praying to neither gods
nor to Buddha,
I am aging
without enlightenment—
today an element of doubt

oh friend who slipped me
from your kimono *sleeve*
a proletarian newspaper,
with the passing of the years
your name too has faded

now I hold dear
this life of mine
which has endured
such busy and eventful times
in 1972

Destiny

1973

冬日

学童ら
降りて来るらし
向山の
林に起こる
朝のさざめき

傾きし
軒の雨垂れ
緩急の
音それぞれに
リズム持ちをり

スピーカーの
<ruby>喚<rt>わめ</rt></ruby>く選挙を
無関心に
聞きつつ蘭の
花芽を数ふ

古びたる
樟の火鉢を
一つ据ゑて
南国の冬
形整ふ

Winter Days

as if school children
have come tumbling down,
this morning a babble
breaks out in the forest
of the mountain across the way

the sounds
of rain dripping
from the slanted eaves,
fast or slow
each has its own rhythm

hearing without interest
an electioneering clamor
through loud-speakers,
I count the buds
on my orchids

placing in my room
an old camphor hand-warmer pot
is the only preparation
I make for winter
in this sub-tropical country

大陸に
帰る日は何時
兵老いて
門辺の荒地に
青菜植ゑをり

一坪の
菜を褒めてより
老兵は
朝会ふ毎に
われに会釈す

進学せぬ
子ならん弁当
ひつ提げ行く
姿日増しに
世故染みて行く

She is my baby
and I'm her baby と
子なきポツパ氏
妻を指しつつ
呵々と笑ふも   （指揮者兼ピアニストポツパ氏とその夫人）

132

when will he
return to the mainland?
an old soldier
is planting greens
in rough ground near the gate

I praise the patch of greens
and the old soldier
bows to me
whenever we meet
in the mornings

he probably didn't finish school,
that lad walking along
with his lunch-box
day after day, getting accustomed
to the ways of the world

'she is my baby
and I'm her baby,'
says the childless Dr. Popper,
pointing at his wife
and laughing haha   (conductor and pianist Dr. Popper and his spouse)

ベトナム和平協定 （一月）

失ひし
ものの多きに
傷心も
新しからん
平和来て更に

誰が為の
十数年の
殺戮か
勝負不明にて
和議成りて行く

The Vietnam Peace Accord (January)

no doubt
there will be
fresh heartbreak
over the many losses,
when peace comes again

for whose sake
have been these decades
of slaughter?
winners and losers unclear,
peace talks are proceeding

老二人

祝はるる
古稀の齢の
　宴なり
上座に夫は
神妙に在り

　躓かず
よろめかずして
ひたすらに
重ねし年よ
我が古稀の夫

親子の分れ住む距離はスープの冷めぬ程度が理想と人は言へど

　スープ冷めぬ
近くに子らは
在らずして
老二人相倚り
静かなる日々

生涯を
悔なき余生
共に生きん
互に残り
少なき月日

Two Old People

a banquet

to celebrate his 70th birthday—

at the head of the table

sits my husband

docilely

he has never stumbled

or staggered

through all these years

of earnest effort—

my seventy-year-old husband

People say that parents and children living separately at a distance is as ideal as soup which has gone cold, but…

the soup has gone cold—

with none of our children

living close by,

these quiet days of two oldies

relying on each other

a life without regrets—

we will live the rest of it

together

mutually supporting each other

through the little time remaining

島の春

_{もた}
擡げ来し
若芽に場をば
譲るごと
楓の老い葉
枝離れ行く

見遙かす
並木の緑
うねりゐて
末は湯町の
靄に融け入る

我よりも
先に牛らは
来るるらし
朝靄の丘に
獣の臭ひ

たわたわと
蜜柑担げる
女らは
足並み揃へ
山を降り来る

138

The Island Spring

as if giving way to
the young buds
held aloft,
the maple tree
is shedding its old leaves

the end of the green billows
on the avenue trees
I see in the distance
dissolving into the steam
from this hot-spring town

it seems the cows
come out earlier than I—
the smell
of these beasts
on the morning-dewed hill

with their loads
of mandarins swaying
and swinging,
women file in step
down the mountain

蜜柑売る
農婦の声は
家々に
皆届きたり
朝の丘町

枯尾花
招く穂先に
きらめける
ダイヤの数よ
春雨の後

雲低く
冷え行く空に
間<ruby>間<rt>ま</rt></ruby>を置きて
起こる爆音
何か不安に

深々と
湯壺に沈み
念ひなし
春嵐時に
窓を揺り行く

in the morning
the voices of farmers' wives
selling mandarins
reaches into every home
in this hill town

after spring rain
the beckoning ears
of withered pampas grass
glitter and gleam
like so many diamonds

I've a sense of unease
at those rumbles
occurring at intervals
in the cooling sky
of low clouds

sinking deeper
into the bath-tub,
no thoughts in my head —
the windows shaking
at times with the spring storm

植ゑ終へし
早苗の列は
<ruby>嬰 児<rt>みどりご</rt></ruby>の
産毛にも似て
風に揺れをり

日影洩る
街路を <ruby>尽<rt>ことごと</rt></ruby> く
埋めたり
楓並木の
いち早き芽立ち

百花の妍
忽ち消えて
一色の
青葉に静もる
南国の春

籠められし
靄ふと切れて
まなかひの
夾竹桃は
<ruby>色鮮<rt>あさ</rt></ruby>らけし

just-planted,
the rows of early rice seedlings
ruffled by the wind
resemble
the hair of a newborn babe

in dappled light and shade,
the maple trees,
great avenues of them
lining all the streets,
sprouting as fast as they can

all of a sudden
the splendor of a hundred flowers
disappears, quietens
into the monocolored green leaves
of this southern land's spring

when the mist
that lay heavily on them
suddenly lifts,
there before my eyes are
the fresh colors of oleanders

Destiny

畑中の
白き人影
点となり
緑の地面を
縫ひつつ移る

春闌けて
娘々廟の
赤き屋根
峡の緑に
僅か残さる

聞き入れば
鳥らおのおの
鳴く方は
決まりあるらし
我が立てる峡

that white-clad figure
in the vegetable fields
becomes a mere dot
sewing green on the ground
as it moves around

when spring is well advanced,
the red roof
of the shrine to the goddesses
is almost invisible
amongst the greenery in the glen

when I enter the glen
and stand there, listening,
it seems as if
each bird has rules
for the way it sings

饒舌な
娘らの語らひか
早口に
鳴く鳥ありて
山辺明るし

声限り
息継ぎもせず
鳴く鳥に
ふと急かれをり
朝の体操

丘に立ち
三十六億の
一人我と
朝の大気を
胸張りて吸ふ

is that the chatter
of talkative young girls?
there are birds
chirping quickly
on the bright mountainside

I'm hurried along
to my morning exercises
by the birds
which sing on and on
without drawing breath

I stand on a hill,
one person among 3.6 billion
who is
expanding her chest, and
breathing in the morning air

渡り来し人ら

バタ屋占めし
廃墟はいつか
とりどりの
襤褸掛かりて
住居と成りぬ

この若き
バタ屋足らひて
あるらんか
黙々と町の
屑集めをる

住みつきて
異質のままに
細々と
暮し立てをり
一群の人

May Yen Ting

People Who Crossed the Sea

some time or other
those deserted ruins occupied
by garbage collectors,
turned into dwellings
hung with all sorts of rags

will it satisfy
this young garbage collector
just silently
gathering up the rubbish
of the town?

coming to dwell here
a group of people
makes a scanty living
in various ways
foreign to them

死者

反骨に
安寧少なき
一生<ruby>一生<rt>ひとよ</rt></ruby>なりき
憾み呑みつつ
遂に終りぬ

何を又
吼<ruby>吼<rt>ほ</rt></ruby>えんとするか
反骨者
息の根絶えても
口開けしまま

来る死者を
オートメの如く
葬儀屋ら
冷凍し行く
市のまんま中　　　　　　　　　　　（台湾は熱帯、且つ準備のかかる土葬なり）

May Yen Ting

The Deceased

a life spent
in rebellion
without tranquility,
swallowing grudges,
has finally ended

I wonder what
he is trying to bellow now?
though the rebel
has stopped breathing
his mouth is open in a roar

in the center of this city,
funeral directors are
mechanically
freezing the remains
of the dead brought to them   (Taiwan is tropical and also customarily has earth
burials, which require a lot of preparation)

初夏

朝靄を
抜き立つ遠^{をち}の
観音山
海に静もる
島影と見る

岩尖^{いはさき}に
白鷺四羽
並びゐて
峡は陽の影
いまだ届かず

相思樹の
黄の花敷ける
坂道を
踏みなづみつつ
爪立てて行く

向山
緑の中に
陽を集め
一樹真黄色の
相思樹の花

Early Summer

thrusting up
through the morning mist
distant Guanyin Mountain
is the very image of
a tranquil island in the sea

on the tip of a rock
four white herons
aligned —
this ravine
is still sunless

hesitating
to step on the yellow flowers
of acacia confusa
carpeting this hill path,
I go along on tiptoe

in the midst of the greenery
on the mountain opposite
sunlight is gathered
on the bright yellow flowers
of an acacia tree

夕茜の
空に鳴き出でしは
まさしくも
初蟬の声
筆擱きて聴く

空罐に
花卉_{くわき}を植ゑつつ
老兵は
する事なしと
吐息して言ふ

手すさびに
兵植ゑしカボチヤ
塀沿ひに
蔓の先端
上げて這ひ行く

come out to sing
in the sky's rosy glow
at evening, surely
they are the first cicadas —
laying down my brush, I listen

setting flowering plants
in an empty can,
the old soldier
heaves a sigh
says he has nothing to do

up along the fence
is creeping the tip of the vine
from that pumpkin
the soldier took pleasure
in planting

時流

世変ると
三十六計
国外に
逃げ足速し
持てる人人

政局に
<ruby>聰<rt>さと</rt></ruby>き人々
<ruby>故国<rt>くに</rt></ruby>棄て行く
いつか一つの
時流となりぬ

May Yen Ting

The Flow of Time

as the world changes,

beating a hasty retreat

overseas

seems the best strategy

to the wealthy

some time or other

it became the fashion

for people

wise to the political situation

to abandon the old country

子らの住むアメリカを訪ふ

三万フィート
機下黎明の
雲海は
揺がぬ巌の
原と映え渡る　　　　　　　　（五月末、子らを訪ねて渡米）

東天に
引かれし一線
燃え行けば
彩の中より
日輪顕ち来ぬ

地の利得んと
異国に播きし
子らの種
時経て変種と
なりしもありぬ

離りるて
子孫らの瑣事
届かざる
安けさ誰か
寂しと言はん

Visiting America Where My Children Live

30,000 feet

below the aircraft

at dawn

a sea of clouds shines

unmoving, like a rocky plain   (going to America to visit my children, at the end of May)

when the line drawn

along the eastern sky

went on fire,

the orb of the sun

rose up from the glow

some seeds my children,

sent to seek profit from the earth,

sowed in foreign lands

may have changed in nature

with the passing of time

some might describe it

as lonely, this freedom

from involvement

in the trivial affairs

of my descendants far away

我が父を
知るやと二歳の
内孫は
海越えて来し
我に聞くかも

異国なる
子らの近きに
家持つとふ
夫の願ひを
　　うべな
　肯ひ兼ねをり

夫の背に
齢あらはなり
執拗に
言ひ来し姿勢
今は言ふまじ

孫守りつつ
中学生の
リーダー読む
口調に夫は
絵本読みをり

you know my Dad?
asks the two-year-old child
of my eldest son,
when I have come
across the sea

I'm unable to assent
to my husband's wish
to have a house
here, near our children
living in this foreign country

my husband's back
shows his age—
I'll not criticize now
the way he persists
in talking

while he minds our grandchild
my husband is reading aloud
a picture book,
in the tones
of a junior high school reader

Destiny

生きるとは
かくぞと思へど
奔命の
子らの姿に
胸ふと疼く　　　　　　　　（アメリカは青・中年らの戦場といふ）

夕テレビ
子供番組に
子ら追ひて
暫し息ぬく
アメリカの母

たかが脚
一本の痛みと
思へども
消え入る程に
もてあましをり　　　　　　（滞米中脚を痛む）

162

May Yen Ting

though I think to myself
'so this is what being alive is like'
I feel a sudden pang
in my heart, at the sight
of my kids' hustle and bustle   (they say America is a battlefield for the young and middle-aged)

American mothers
can take a breather for a bit
while their kids
follow the programs
on evening television

pain only in one leg
not too much of a problem,
I thought,
but I felt quite faint
it was so unbearable   (the sore leg I experienced while staying America)

アラスカの旅 （六月）

追はれ来て
苛酷な自然
条件に
アラスカインデイアン
今も生きつぐ

さい果てに
追はれ幾世の
インデイアンの
子ら黒々と
大きな眸

年行かぬ
インデイアンの子らの
手踊りよ
欠伸も見せつ
床踏まへるる

インデイアンの
子ら踊り終ふるや
桶持ちて
出口に客の
チツプを待ちをり

May Yen Ting

A Trip to Alaska (June)

chased away,
the Alaskan Indians
even now
keep on living
in harsh natural conditions

driven to the border's edge
and surviving
over several generations,
Indian children
with their big black eyes

still quite young,
Indian children perform
their 'hand dance'
yawning from time to time
as they tread the boards

the dancing
of the Indian kids finishes —
holding tubs
they wait at the exit
for tips from the audience

チップの多寡
読みてるるらし
インディアンの
子捧ぐる桶を
ふと覗きたり

民族の
思ひ総てを
垂直な
柱一本に
彫りて立てたり　　　　　　　　（トーテムポール）

厳寒に
堪へて幾世の
山の樅^{もみ}の
木梢^{こうれ}さい果ての
天に突き入る

アラスカや
枯木の高きに
鷲一羽
夕づく海に
向きて動かず

apparently checking out
the amount of tips,
the Indian kids
suddenly peered into
the tubs they were holding

the feelings and thoughts
of their race
all carved
onto one vertical pillar,
standing there   (a totem pole)

withstanding severe cold,
growing for generations
in the mountains
fir trees pierce the sky
at the end of the earth

oh, Alaska...
high on a dead tree
an eagle
in the evening
faces the sea, motionless

夕冷えの
海に輪になり
代る代る
波を乗り飛ぶ
アラスカ千鳥

何処指し
ゆく鳥群か
小さき羽
頻りに打ちて
大洋を行く

寒々と
佗しさのみの
アラスカよ
地球の皺の
寄せたる所

白雪の
連峯厳に
はだかりて
アラスカ今も
人を拒絶す

making rings
on the evening-cooled sea,
a succession of Alaskan plovers
riding the waves
then flying off

to where is
that flock of birds pointing?
flapping tiny wings
incessantly
they fly over the ocean

oh, Alaska
nothing but cold, cold
desolation,
a place where the world
is all creased

white snow
over the majestic spread
of mountain peaks—
the Alaska that even now
rebuffs human kind

人知れず
幾世積み来し
大氷河
機下に迫りて
凝視を拒む

氷河湾
波に散り敷く
氷塊は
緑野に映ゆる
白き花列か

乗客の
暇潰さんと
プログラム
盛りだくさんの
アラスカ船旅

深夜のショウ
終ればデッキに
連峯の
暮色を愛づる
極北の旅

it has not known people
for several centuries now
the great glacier
lying below our aircraft
defies our staring eyes

those ice floes
scattered over the waves
of Glacier Bay, are
somehow like rows of white flowers
reflecting the green plains

on the Alaskan cruise
heaps and heaps
of planned activities
to kill time
for the passengers

voyage to the extreme north:
when the midnight show is over,
up on deck we admire
the evening colors
on the chain of mountain peaks

雪かづく
夏山を背に
海に沿ふ
家皆小さし
アラスカの首都

富士の嶺と
相似の火山
その別称
アラスカシツカの
フジヤマといふ

幾世紀
経たる氷河の
一角の
崩落して<ruby>飛沫<rt>ひ まつ</rt></ruby>
海に吸はるる

at their backs
summer mountains covered in snow,
houses in the Alaskan capital
along the coast
all looking so small

that volcano
resembling the peak
of Mt. Fuji,
has an alternate name:
Alaska Sitka's Fujiyama

after many centuries
one corner of the glacier
has broken away
and fallen, its spray
swallowed by the sea

Destiny

北欧の旅 <small>(八月)</small>

緑園の
百花の如し
空よりの
北欧の町は
揃ひの赤屋根

アラスカに
凹み行きしか
スカンジナヴィア
国国波に
漂ふ如く

デンマークは一つの半島と五百近い島より成る

デンマーク
浮き洲と畑と
幾何模様
描きて眼下に
一つ又一つ

毛を刈られし
羊の背か
ノールウェイ
木は皆低く
岩肌見ゆる

174

A Trip to Northern Europe (August)

like a hundred flowers

in green gardens,

seen from the sky

the towns of northern Europe

with their uniform red roofs

did they go sagging

into Alaska—

the countries

of Scandinavia

seem to float on the waves

Denmark is comprised of one peninsula and close to five hundred islands.

Denmark:

floating islands and fields

in geometric patterns

laid out under my eyes

one after another

are those the backs

of shorn sheep?

the trees in Norway

look all low-growing,

in rocky ground

Destiny

スカンジナヴィア
老山脉の
丸き背に
絣模様の
残雪まばら

幾戦を
経て建てられし
国ならん
辻の銅像
皆馬上の将軍　　　　　　（スエーデン・ストックホルム）

ソ連より
解放されて
年経るに
表情硬し
フィンランドの人ら

on the round backs
of old mountain ranges
in Scandinavia
patches of remaining snow
like the Japanese kasuri *pattern*

this nation
must have been established
after many wars...
on street corners, bronze statues
all of generals on horseback　　　(Stockholm, Sweden)

though years have passed
since their liberation
from the Soviet Union,
the Finnish people
still have stiff expressions

Destiny

一九五二年オリンピック大会ここヘルシンキに於て挙行され、人見絹枝嬢一九二六
年スウエーデンの万国女子オリンピック大会と一九二八年オランダのオリンピック
大会に於て輝かしき成績を挙ぐ、二五歳にて歿す

ここに来て

名揚げし人ら

今何処

オリソピックスタジアム

寂として残る

今在らば

我と同年の

人見嬢

健闘の跡に

来て胸痛む

コッペンハーゲン

日本館とふに

飛び入りて

平げし飯^{めし}

一櫃^{ひとひつ}の味　　　　　　　　　　（デンマーク）

説教聴くも

行^{ぎやう}の一つか

大寺院^{キャシードラル}

椅子の背の棒

居眠り防ぐと　　　　　　　　　（クロンボルグの古城）

In 1952 the Olympic Games were held here, in Helsinki; Ms. Hitomi Kinue, who achieved brilliant results at the 1926 Sweden Multinational Women's Olympics and at the 1928 Olympic Games in Holland, died at the age of twenty-five.

those people who

came here and gained fame,

where are they now?

the Olympic stadium

remains in solitary splendor

were she alive today,

Ms. Hitomi would be

the same age as I—

at this place of her achievements

my heart aches

oh, the taste

of that tub of rice I devoured

when I rushed

to the 'Japan Hall'

in Copenhagen　　　　　　(Denmark)

is listening to the sermon

part of religious training?

on the backs of the chairs

in the Cathedral, a bar

to prevent dozing, I'm told　　　(old Kronborg Castle)

Destiny

師を訪ふ

九月下旬米国より婦台して約一箇月後十月二十二日に東京に赴き四賀師を訪問す

　近く師に
　まみゆる我と
　朝夕の
　冷えにもわけて
　身をいとひをり

　師にまみゆる
　念ひ一筋に
　三千キロ
　秋空をひた
　飛びに飛び行く

Visiting My Teacher

Towards the end of September, I returned from America to Taiwan, and about a month later, on October 22, I went to Tokyo to visit my teacher, Shiga-sensei.

I'll be seeing my teacher

very soon, so I am

taking care of myself

especially in the chill

of morning and evening

with the single thought

of meeting my teacher

I'm flying in earnest,

3,000 kilometers

through the autumn sky

我が伯母

礦山町の
いぶせきに我が伯母
纒足続け
矍鑠として
<ruby>矍鑠<rt>かくしゃく</rt></ruby>として
九十五年生く

何の風に
吹かれ来しかと
我が稀な
訪れを伯母
すかさずに斬る

背丸まり
小さくなりし
伯母ひそと
扉の陰に一日
<ruby>扉<rt>と</rt></ruby>の陰に一日
珠数を爪ぐる

死とはかく
随時にあるとふ
証かや
<ruby>証<rt>あかし</rt></ruby>かや
医者義兄自らも
<ruby>医者義兄<rt>あに</rt></ruby>自らも
予期せぬ最期

May Yen Ting

My Aunt

my aunt
who lives in a shabby place
in a mining town,
hale and hearty at ninety-five
still with bound feet

what wind has
blown you here, I wonder,
is the swift,
cutting response of my aunt
to this rare visit I make

my aunt, become tiny
and hump-backed, sits all day
in the shadow of a door
privately and quietly
fingering her rosary beads

is this proof that death
can come thus, at any time?
her passing now
was unforeseen even
by my brother-in-law, a doctor

秋の陽

雲間の陽
実りし向うの
棚田のみ
黄金の色に
しかと截ち切る

朝道を
掃く老人は
一山の
落葉片方に
新聞読みゐる

アラーに伏す
白衣の群か
一望の
尾花は風に
背を屈めをり

Autumn Sunshine

from among the clouds, the sun

draws a clear line

lighting with gold

only the ripened paddies

across the way

the old man

who sweeps the morning path,

is reading a newspaper

beside a huge mound

of fallen leaves

is that a crowd

of white-clad men

prostrating themselves before Allah?

a whole swathe of pampas grass

bending over in the wind

中東の戦ひ

中束の
子供喧嘩に
陰の親
ちらりちらりと
顔見せてをり

子供喧嘩
大人の喧嘩に
成り行くか
中東のニュース
息詰めて聴く

May Yen Ting

The Middle East Conflict

children quarrelling

in the Middle East—

now and then

in the shadows glimpses

of their parents' faces shown

are children's quarrels

becoming adults' quarrels?

holding my breath

I listen to the news

about the Middle East

資源

中東の
戦ひ石油に
飛火して
我が身辺を
じりじりと焼く

資源なき
国の弱さよ
はるばると
腰折りて行く
アラビア詣で

友好は
<ruby>中 位<rt>ちゅうぐらる</rt></ruby>とふ
序列にて
アラーの油を
押し頂くも

油の火
絶えし寒さに
目覚めたり
経済大国
一朝の夢

Resources

the conflict in the Middle East
is spreading to petroleum —
little by little
my surroundings
start to be grilled

oh, the weakness
of nations with no natural resources —
they go cap in hand
to faraway Arabia
begging for oil

the friendship rating
is only 'medium'
even when
Arabian petroleum
is received reverently

no more oil for heating,
I wake in the cold —
a morning dream
of those economic
'super-powers'

亡き父が
一生<ruby>一生<rt>ひとよ</rt></ruby>をかけし
石炭また
陽の目見る世か
いつまで続く

事業とて
<ruby>狸掘り<rt>たぬきぼ</rt></ruby>の<ruby>坑<rt>こう</rt></ruby>
たやすげに
這ひて行きたる
父若かりき

狸掘りの
坑を這ひつつ
行く父の
地下足袋消えて
坑暗かりし

狸掘り
石炭<ruby>一箕<rt>いっき</rt></ruby>の
繩腰に
礦夫は坑を
這ひ出でて来ぬ

that coal
my deceased father
used all his life…
will it be seeing
the light of day, again?

doing his job,
my father when young
crawled with ease
round the mines, digging
in better parts for better yield

while he crawled
through the pits digging
in a special way
my father's underground socks
vanished in the mine's darkness

some of the miners
who dug that special way
for better coal,
came crawling out of the pit,
with bags roped to them

近親身辺

子孫らに
別れ告げんと
癌病める
姪大洋を
独り飛び行きぬ

コバルトの
照射に指も
曲りぬと
言ふ姪の手紙
判じつつ読む

健康なりし
日を憶ひこの
痛む手が
なければと思ふ
姪の書きし文

出張終へ
立ち寄りし子を
留めずして
遠き妻子の
許に急がせぬ　　　　　　（末の子）

Happenings Among My Close Relatives

to farewell
her descendants, my niece
suffering from cancer
flew alone
across the Pacific

reading my niece's letter,
I work out that
she is saying
her fingers have been bent
by the cobalt ray treatment

remembering the days
when she was healthy,
she wishes
her hands weren't so sore,
my niece wrote in her letter

business trip completed,
my son dropped by to see me —
I didn't ask him to stay,
but urged him to return
to his distant wife and children   *(my youngest son)*

若きらが
離職し行く世に
古稀の夫
咎<ruby>持つ如く<rt>とが</rt></ruby>
ポスト占めをり

三十寡婦の
姑が五人の
子育てし
記録に幾度
涙抑ふる　　　　　　　　　（姑生誕百年の記念帳を編む）

あてがはれし
玩具の犬と
遊ぶなり
曾ての闘士
老い果てて日々

194

in a world whose

young people quit their jobs,

my seventy-year-old husband

is sticking to his post

as if charged with it

reading the record

of the five children

raised by the mother-in-law

of a thirty-year-old widow,

I hold back my tears   (compiling a commemorative book for my mother-in-law's hundredth birthday)

once a fighter,

this man, old and frail

at the end of his life

plays with the toy dog

provided every day

1974

日本語の本をい編む

一生かけて
培ひて来し
日本語を
異国語として
子に孫に教ふ

我が血肉と
なりし日本語
伝へんと
心こめつつ
編みぬ幾冊

宿願の
日本語の本
編み上げて
千九百七十三年と
ピリオドを打つ

文例に
金といふ文字
多かりし
我が旧き著書
日本語の読本

Compiling Japanese Language Books

this Japanese cultivated

over my lifetime

I teach now

as a foreign language

to my children and grandchildren

the Japanese language,

my blood and bones…

determined

to pass it on, I put together

several books

as I'd dreamed of doing,

I compiled the books

of Japanese,

finishing them off

in 1973

in the sentence patterns

of those Japanese reading books

I authored long ago,

the character for 'money'

appears many times

冷冬

冷冬が
染め上げたるか
蔦もみぢ
向ひの石壁
燃ゆるばかりに

ま向ひの
垣の蔦もみぢ
校正に
疲れてはふと
目を遣るところ

朝庭に
見出でし無数の
梅の蕾
誰にか告げん
心弾むも

Chilly Winter

has the chilly winter
dyed the scarlet-tinged ivy?
it seems to burn
on the stone wall
of the house opposite

when my eyes
grow tired from proof-reading
I shift them
to the scarlet-tinged ivy
right opposite

when I discovered
in the morning garden
countless buds on the plum tree,
my heart was bursting
with the desire to tell someone

麗日（れいじつ）も
梅満開も
めでたさの
うちに数へぬ
老二人の元朝　　　　　　　　　（旧暦の正月）

庭先にて
先づ梅の花
愛（め）でさせて
後（のち）招じ入れぬ
年始の客を

beautiful weather,
a plum tree in full bloom,
among the blessings
we two oldies counted
on New Year's morning   (the Lunar New Year)

New Year's guests —
first of all, the plum blossoms
in our garden
to be enjoyed, then
we invited them inside

春の萌し

並木路
若芽の脱ぎし
鱗苞が
一条白く
丘に伸び行く

移り行く
季におくれたる
玉椿
下枝の蕾
尚堅きまま

襲ひ来し
余寒に庭の
静まれる
椿再び
急ぎ咲きつぐ

May Yen Ting

Signs of Spring

up the hill
stretches a white ribbon
of 'bract scales'
shed by the new buds
in the avenue of trees

late to bloom
in this changing season
buds on the lower branches
of the precious camellia
are still tightly closed

the garden grows quiet
under the left-over cold
attacking it,
but the camellia hastens
to come back into bloom

憶ひ出

畦^{あぜ}沿ひの
小川入りて
蝦^{えび}取りつつ
使ひに行きし
幼^{をさな}かりし日

腹の上を
這ひ行く小亀
見しと夜半
父を起こせり
幼かりし日

夢うつつ
われ見しと呼ぶ
小亀をば
父はランプを
掲げて探せし

Memories

in my youth, I would
get into the stream
running along the ridge
to fish for prawns —
even while out on errands

when very young
I once woke my father
at midnight, saying
I saw a little tortoise
crawling on my belly

I called my father,
and holding a lamp
he searched for
the little tortoise I said
had appeared in my dream

庭藪に
熟るる無花果
尽くるまで
人に秘めるし
われ少女の日

我が婚に
母の給ひし
庖丁は
痩せ果てて尚
光を放つ

once, as a girl,
I hid from people
until all the figs
ripening in our orchard
had been consumed

the cleaver
given to me by my mother
for my marriage,
still gleams, though
it has worn very thin

遠来の友

三月初旬植松節子様乗台

待ち得たる
友にま向ひ
喜びは
言葉とならず
ただ声揚ぐる

遠来の
友に招宴
断はらせ
己が家内（やぬち）の
くらし見て貰ふ

奇縁ぞと
想ひを語り
日常の
くらしも見せつ
この友の前

香を頼り
見上げ見上げて
確かめし
実生（みしやう）ザボンの
初花小さき

A Friend Comes From Afar

In early March, Uematsu Setsuko-sama came to Taiwan.

confronted with the friend
I had been waiting for,
unable to express
my joy in words, I just
uttered some sounds

declining an invitation
to the party of my friend
who had come from afar,
I took pleasure
in showing her my home life

telling her I felt
this was a stroke of fate
I displayed
to my friend
my everyday lifestyle

drawn by their fragrance,
I looked up higher
and checked — yes
the first little blooms were there,
on the shaddock grown from seed

日本の新聞

上官の
空しき命^{めい}を
一筋に
兵ジャングルに
ありし三十年　　　　　　　（小野田寛郎氏現る）

兵といふ
人間像を
幻に
三十余年
時世の推移

相つぎて
起こる日本の
大ニュース
空輸の新聞に
生々^{なま}と読む

May Yen Ting

Japanese Newspapers

for thirty years
never deviating
from the useless orders
of his senior officer,
that soldier lived in the jungle   (*Onoda Hirō appears*)

though the world moved on,
for thirty long years
he kept the illusion
of being a soldier
as his human image

there's a succession
of major news' stories
coming out of Japan —
I read the latest bulletins
in the airmail editions

日々空輸の
新聞を読む
幸_{さち}ありて
日本に暫し
心遊ばす

師の在_います
鎌倉の記事
新聞に
心して読む
習ひとなりし

everyday
I read the newspaper
delivered by air,
lucky to be able to enjoy
Japan for a while

I've got into the habit
of taking care to read
any newspaper articles
about Kamakura
where my teacher lives

断絶

我が国籍
移りて過去の
修養は
異質の如く
裡に凝りぬ

各世代
各異国語の
我が家族
歴史のままに
断絶に慣る

Severance

my nationality changed,
the disciplines of the past
are latent
inside me
like something alien

for each generation
a different foreign language…
like history itself
my family accustomed to
gaps in communication

帰省の孫ら

遊びふと
悪戯^{わるさ}となりて
挑^{いど}み来る
　幼^{をさな}孫らに思ふ
彼等との距離

我が顔を
読みつつ障子に
穴明ける
幼孫らに
無視もて応ず

幼孫の
食べさせくるる
アイスクリームに
口を持ち行く
公園のベンチ

我が口に
アイスクリームを
送る時
己が口をも
孫は開けをり

May Yen Ting

The Grandchildren's Homecoming

young grandkids, a challenge
when their playing suddenly
turns to naughtiness,
making me conscious
of the distance between us

my small grandchild
looks for a reaction in my face
as he pokes holes
in the paper screen —
I respond by ignoring him

sitting a park bench,
I bring my mouth
close to the ice cream
my small grandchild
wants to feed me

delivering the ice cream
into my mouth,
the grandchild
opens his own mouth
simultaneously

片目づつ
我と弟の
それぞれの
縄飛び見よと
孫にせがまる

孫去りて
その残したる
ヤドカリも
幾日我らが
語らひの種

孫共に
置かれ行きたる
ヤドカリを
かたへに歌稿
書き急ぎをり

my granddaughter urges me
to watch them both
skipping rope,
with one eye on her, and
one on her younger brother

grandchildren departed,
that hermit crab
still here
provides a source of conversation
for us for a few days

I'm hurrying
to write a tanka *manuscript,*
putting aside
that hermit crab
our grandkids left behind

御所柿

実生柿の
初生りを
日に幾度も
出でて確かむ
五月雨の中

花咲くとも
見えざりし御所柿
高枝に
小さき青果
早や形なす

迷ひ来し
草蟬一つ
放たんと
そと手に取れば
幼声揚ぐ

Gosho Persimmons

in the early summer rain
I go out many times each day
to check on the first fruit
of that persimmon tree
I've grown from seed

it did not even seem to bloom,
yet already
on high branches
of the Gosho *persimmon tree*
small green fruits are formed

thinking to free
the grass cicada which has
come here by mistake,
I gently take it in my hand
whereupon it gives a young cry

落つべき実
落ち尽しけん
実生柿
残り若干に
心安らぐ

相思樹の
落花<ruby>細<rt>らくくわ</rt></ruby>かに
織り込みて
庭の芝生は
鬱金のカーペット

all of the fruit

bound to fall, has fallen, I think—

to my relief some remains

on this persimmon tree

grown from seed

flowers fallen

from the acacia

are weaving

into the lawn of our garden

a delicate golden carpet

日本宣言

日航機台湾を飛ばずといふ

追ひ出され
切り捨てられて
果て如何に
なり行く島か
我等の運命

片や島
片や大陸
天秤に
かけて方向
決めしか日航機

ドル箱の
航路振り捨てて
見せんとす
弱小国の
五分の魂

運命を
宣告さるる
如く読む
日本紙上の
台湾の記事

226

The Japanese Declaration

I hear that JAL planes will not fly to Taiwan.

what will become
of this island, ultimately?
having been chased away
and then abandoned,
what are we destined for?

the fate of this island
hangs in the balance
with the mainland—
will Japan Airlines
decide which way to go?

'even a worm will turn,'
this small, weak country
tries to demonstrate
by abandoning
the money-making air route

I read this
as a declaration of our destiny,
the article
in the Japanese newspaper
about Taiwan

長き過去の
縁を一気に
切り捨てつ
三行半の
日本宣言

漢薬煮る
匂ひ流れて
移り来し
隣家夫人の
顔まだ知らず

百年も
生き得る如し
しかじかの
計画を言ふ
夫に相槌打たず

at one blow severing the ties
of a long, shared past,
this Japanese Declaration
has the terseness
of a letter of divorce

the smell of Chinese herbs
being boiled for medicine
comes flowing into our place,
but I still haven't met
the neighboring woman

as if we are going to be able
to live for a hundred years,
my husband outlines to me
this plan and that—
I make no comments

飢餓

飢餓来るとふ
地球に住まふ
孫共の
未来思へば
憂ひ果てなし

幾億の
民饉じうても
アトミックボムと
判断せしか
ガンジー総理

Famine

famines are coming, they say
to this world where
my grandchildren live—
when I think about their future,
my anxiety knows no bounds

did several millions
of starving people
decide on
the atomic bomb,
President Gandhi?

盛夏

椰子の樹に
身をそらせつつ
蟬徐々に
殻脱ぎ行きぬ
上弦の月

雨の絶え間
絶え間の日照る
空押して
鳴きとよむもよ
蟬の声々

孫らへと
手植ゑし果樹の
初生りを
巡り見てより
ひと日始まる

ポーチの上の
葡萄幾房
透明に
なり行く色を
朝夕楽しむ

High Summer

leaning back
against the palm tree
a cicada
was gradually shedding its husk
under the waxing moon

between intervals
in rain showers
the sun shines, and
the chirring of cicadas
resounds against the sky

I start the day
with walking round surveying
the first produce from fruit trees
I have planted by hand
for my grandchildren

some bunches of grapes
hanging over the porch
are growing transparent—
morning and evening
I enjoy their colors

故里福州

福州の
杉柱いや
太きまま
廃屋となりぬ
故里の家

夕づく陽
地平に落ちて
畑中の
_{はは}
姑の墓標を
風揺りて行く

姑の墓所に
水牛幾つ
遊びるて
昼の畑野は
人影もなし

May Yen Ting

The Old Village, Fuzhou

though the cedar pillars
of Fuzhou
remain as thick as ever,
the house in our old village
is now deserted

as the setting sun
drops to the horizon,
wind trembles across the marker
of my mother-in-law's grave
in the middle of the field

by my mother-in-law's grave
several water buffalo
are idling —
no human shadow
falls on the noonday field

無事息災

見えは言はず
荒仕事にも
尚堪ふる
体力持てば
心満ち足る

精一杯
生きし 証か
節くれて
先丸まりし
十本の指

有名人
ならねど事なく
生き来しを
今はひたすら
身の幸と思はん

死出の装束
夏干ししてゐし
母よその
母の年頃
我早や過ぎぬ

A Calm Passing Away

I don't mean to boast,
but when I still
have the strength
to bear this physical work,
my heart will be fully content

is this proof
that I have lived life
to the full?
the joints of my ten fingers
are gnarled, their tips rounded

although I am not
a famous person,
I think of it now
truly as my good fortune
to have lived safely thus far

oh my mother,
I remember you in summer
drying out attire for the dead —
I have already passed
the age you were then

訪米

日本を経由してアメリカに行くとて師の歌の「白き湾」を求む

白き湾
いづこ羽田に
機首指せば
<ruby>汀<rt>みぎは</rt></ruby> の屈折
眼下にしるし

我が機首の
指せる下空に
<ruby>長梅雨<rt>ながつゆ</rt></ruby>の
雲か <ruby>巖<rt>いはほ</rt></ruby> と
<ruby>凝<rt>こ</rt></ruby>りて動かず

汚染言ふ
東都の空に
落日は
<ruby>光芒<rt>くわうばう</rt></ruby>収めて
いよいよ赤し

ポートランドの
住宅地区に
移り来て
夫の高声
気にしつつ住む　　　　（仮寓三箇月）

Visiting America

As I was going to America via Japan, I sought my teacher's *tanka* collection, 'The White Bay.'

where is the white bay?
when the head of my plane
points to Haneda,
the indented shore
below our eyes is white

in the lower sky, where
the head of my plane points,
are those clouds
from the long rainy season,
like an outcrop of rocks, unmoving?

over Tokyo
in the so-called polluted skies,
the setting sun
delivering shafts of light
is redder and redder

we have moved
to a residential district
in Portland,
living there while I worry
about my husband's loud voice   *(three months' temporary residence)*

239

裏庭を
限る疎らな
樅立木
彼我のプライバシー
分たるるところ

プヲイバシーは
垂れしカーテンの
向うなり
塀をよろはぬ
アメリカの家

住む主の
心を読み行く
思ひ思ひに
趣向こらせる
道沿ひの庭

キッチン設備
数の操作も
煩し
老いて営む
アメリカ生活

a sparse stand
of silver fir trees
bordering the back garden
separates the private space
for both sides

privacy is on the other side
of the hanging curtains —
these American houses
are not reliant
on walls

we're learning about
the owners' personalities
by viewing their gardens,
each with its individual design,
alongside the road

the operation by numbers
of this kitchen equipment
is troublesome
for us old people to manage
in our American life

味噌汁の
匂ひキッチンに
ひろごりて
郷愁覚ゆ
異国の暮し

子孫<ruby>子<rt>こ</rt>孫<rt>ま</rt>ら<rt>ご</rt></ruby>らと
あれど異質の
国に住む
この孤独感
我のみのもの

かけひきの
要を子に説く
夫の声
いつか責めるる
口調となりぬ

the aroma
of miso soup spreads
through the kitchen
making us nostalgic
amid our foreign living

though I do have
children and grandchildren,
they live in an alien land —
this solitary feeling
is mine alone

the voice of my husband
explaining to our son
the need for negotiation,
in the end took on
an accusatory tone

転落

自由欲る
民らの怒り
極まりて
放ちし弾か
朴氏目がけて

夫故の
そば杖受けて
ファストレディ
橙のチマ一瞬
朱に染まりつ

日本への
デモに名残りの
鉢巻して
揉みつつい行く
ソウルの民衆

根のよき
弾劾に椅子
揺すられて
ニクソン降りたり
民主国アメリカ

Downfall

aimed at Mr. Park Chung-hee,
were those shots fired off
in the extremity
of anger, by people
desirous of their freedom?

the 'First Lady'
alongside her husband
when he was shot,
her orange skirt
instantly dyed red

people in Seoul
demonstrating against Japan
wear traditional headbands
as they zig-zag
running along

with persistent impeachment
his chair was rocked
and Nixon
tumbled down
in democratic America

揉み消す程

火の手上がりて

ニクソンは

命奪（と）られぬ

水門事件（ウォーターゲート）

絶頂より

落ちて深手の

ニクソンに

尚容赦なき

法の追ひ打ち

孫らの供をしてポートランド動物園に遊ぶ

リズミカルに

ただ足踏みを

繰り返す

機械となれり

檻中の象

百獣の

王の威容は

いづこぞや

四肢天に向け

眠りこけをり

a fire started
which had to be smothered —
Nixon
was robbed of his life
after the Watergate incident

fallen from the summit,
severely wounded,
Nixon is still
mercilessly
hounded by the law

Accompanied by our grandchildren, we enjoy a day at the Portland zoo.

the elephant
in its enclosure
become a mere machine,
stamping over and over
rhythmically

where is the majesty
of the hundred beasts?
with his four limbs
pointed up in the air,
the lion is fast asleep

彗星<ruby>するせい</ruby>に

似し与謝野女史

さりながら

恒に光ります

我が師光る子　　　　　　　　（四賀師の「老いの花」のお言葉を読みて）

飯食む習ひ

この国に

飢餓の日なからん

公園に

路傍<ruby>ろばう</ruby>に果実

生<ruby>な</ruby>るまま落つるまま

コロンビア河の支流に鮭帰り来ぬ

戻り来し

鮭よ銀鱗

失せ果てて

冷たき川瀬に

息絶えるたり

裏藪に

来鳴く烏に

醒されぬ

北辺遅き

明けのまどろみ

248

my teacher, the Bright One

shines always

as did

the comet-like poetess,

Yosano Akiko   *(on reading the expressions of Shiga-sensei in 'Old Flowers')*

Eating Habits

in this country

there must be no times

of starvation —

by the paths in the park

ripe fruit lies where it has fallen

Salmon have returned to the tributaries of the Columbia river.

oh those returned salmon!

they have ended up

losing their silver scales,

breathing their last breaths,

in the chilled shallows

as I dozed at dawn

in the late northern sunrise,

I was woken

by birds come to sing

in the grove behind

路沿ひに
生^なりゐる
赤き酸漿^{ほほづき}に
呼び醒されし
杳き少女期

ふと心
弾みて一気に
登りたる
丘は紫苑^{しをん}の
花の紫

天辺に
躍る銀鱗か
光りつつ
揉み合ひさやぐ
白ポプラの葉

咲き盛^{さか}る
大輪支へて
揺^{ゆる}がざり
青芝に立つ
向日葵の茎

recollections
of my distant girlhood, come
when I find
growing by the roadside
red Chinese lantern fruit

seeing on the hill
climbed at one go
the purple
of aster flowers,
I felt my heart leap

are those silver fish scales
dancing in the heavens?
sparkling and jostling
the rustling leaves
of a white poplar tree

supporting their great heads
in prolific bloom
sunflower stalks
stand motionless
on the green lawn

人気なき
住宅地区を
己れ独り
負ひゐる如し
大き向日葵

蒲公英の
花絮ふと崩れて
向き向きに
漂ひ行きぬ
夕陽の野中

門辺占むる
芒一叢
ふとぶとと
穂を噴き上げて
遠目に眩し

飯を食む
習ひ今なほ
持ちてをり
アメリカ市民と
なりし我が子ら

those huge sunflowers
look as if they alone
are responsible
for the emptiness
of this residential area

a dandelion's seed ball
suddenly fell apart
and fragments went floating
in different directions
through the sunset field

a dense clump of pampas grass
that occupies the space
near the gates,
spouting ears now
dazzles the distant eye

even though my children
have now become
American citizens,
they still continue our custom
of eating rice meals

仕込まれし
「阿公・阿媽好!」を
（アコン　アマアハオ）
歌ふごと
言ひに来る孫を
今日も待ちをり　　　　　　　　　（「お祖父さんお祖母さん今日は」の意味）

洗ひやる
孫に英語の
発音を
正されてをり
浴槽の中

老いては子に従ふのみならず孫にも従ふ

言はさるる
まま児の発音を
まねるたり
師に就く如く
口まねるたり

三箇月の旅終りて故家に落ちつく

助け合ひ
辛じて一人前の
老二人
旅の無事もて
今年の納め

today again we're waiting
for the coming of our grandson,
who says, like he has been taught
"Akon, Ama, hao"
as if he is singing   *(that means "Hello, Grandpa and Grandma")*

my English pronunciation
is corrected
by the grandchild
I am washing
in the bathtub

Old age means not only obeying our children, but also obeying our grandchildren.

I was copying
the child's pronunciation
just the way he spoke,
copying with my mouth
like following a teacher

Relaxing at our old house after three months' traveling

we two oldies,
fully-fledged travelers, were
able to get around
with barely any help:
this year's gift from the gods

秋冬の交

朝の我が
体操の場を
じりじりと
狭め奪(と)りたり
丘野の芒

藪中に
笛の音に鳴く
鳥のあり
声馴染み来て
姿まだ見せぬ

飛行雲
目路の限りに
秋空の
青をくつきり
截(た)ちて行きたり

アパートに
飼はるる鳥の
鳴き交はす
声は鋭く
あたりに透る

May Yen Ting

Autumn into Winter

the pampas grasses
in this field on the hill
press tightly round me,
narrowing the space
for my morning exercises

in the grove
are birds which sing like flutes—
accustomed as I am
to their voices,
I've never yet sighted them

a contrail
drawing a clear line
as far as the eye could see
in the azure
of the autumn sky

shrill, almost piercing,
the sound from the voices
of the tame birds
kept in that apartment,
as they sing to each other

下し来る
一陣毎の
風の音
夜半に目覚めて
聴き分けてをり

短日に
暑気戻り来て
宵早く
夜来香が
甘く匂ひぬ

指切りする
如く再会
約したり
五十年ぶり
会ひに来し友　　　　　　　　　（北海道よりの友）

ニクソンに
倣ひ敲かれて
気早くも
田中総理は
椅子を降りたり　　　　　　（ニクソンは年余頑張りしが）

May Yen Ting

at midnight I wake
and listen to the wind,
hearing
each gust distinctly
as it comes blowing down

on these winter-short days,
the heat has returned —
early in the evening
I smell the sweet fragrance
of tuberoses

like making a pledge
by hooking fingers,
we promised to meet again —
I and the friend who'd come
to see me after fifty years   *(my friend from Hokkaido)*

following Nixon,
Prime Minister Tanaka
pounded with criticism
hurriedly decided
to step down   *(though Nixon held on for more than a year)*

Destiny

大木の
三省堂を
吹き倒しぬ
不況の風は
極東日本へも　　　　　　　（三省堂倒産）

達磨大師
それより長く
モロタイの
山に向ひて
修めし行か　　　　　　　　（中村輝夫伍長）

幻の
如く出で来し
残兵に
掻きたてられる
戦の古創

260

the stout tree of Sanseido
has been blown down —
the winds of recession
have reached the Far East,
even Japan   (bankruptcy of Sanseido bookstore)

facing the mountain
of Morotai,
did Nakamura
perform Buddhist devotions
longer than the Great Teacher Daruma? (Corporal Nakamura Teruo)

that soldier left behind
has reappeared
like a phantom,
causing quite a stir
reopening old war wounds

帰り来し
故国は人間の
ジャングルにて
住みがたかりしか
ブラジルにゆきし　　　　　　（小野田寛郎少尉）

<ruby>蝕<rt>しょく</rt></ruby><ruby>甚<rt>じん</rt></ruby>の
月<ruby>後夜<rt>ごや</rt></ruby>に光
帰り来て
天の<ruby>奥処<rt>おくど</rt></ruby>に
小さく冴ゆる

索かれ行く
豚の悲鳴は
明けやらぬ
<ruby>峡<rt>かひ</rt></ruby>の暁闇に
しばし響かふ

May Yen Ting

the old country
he came back to
is a 'human jungle' —
was it difficult to live in,
so he went to Brazil?   (Second Lieutenant Onoda Hirō)

after the maximum eclipse
of the moon, light returns
early in the morning
while in the depths of the sky
the moon shines small but clear

the squeals of the pig
dragged along with a rope,
echo for a long while
in the pre-dawn darkness
of the valley

Destiny

1975

報歳蘭

咲きそむと
見るまに本咲きと
なり行きて
年頭に映す
わが庭桜

立てば匂ひ
坐れば匂ふ
机の上の
報歳蘭に
<ruby>報歳蘭<rt>ベウスエイラン</rt></ruby>に
歌作すすまず

貼り換へし
<ruby>障子清々し<rt>すがすが</rt></ruby>
今日もまた
<ruby>書読みさして<rt>ふみ</rt></ruby>
<ruby>前に来て佇つ<rt>た</rt></ruby>

May Yen Ting

The Cymbidium Orchid

just as it seemed
to be starting to flower,
the cherry tree
burst into full bloom,
beautiful in our New Year's garden

standing or sitting
I can smell the fragrance
of the cymbidium orchid
on my desk—yet I make
no progress writing tanka

where I've replaced paper
on the shōji, *they look cool*
and crisp, today too
I stop reading books
to stand in front of the shōji

Destiny

不況下の
ジャンボ機故国へ
売り込みに
子は帰りたり
二十三年ぶり

眼裏に
今もまざまざ
戸山ケ原
弟連れて
凧揚げし子よ

268

May Yen Ting

for the first time
in twenty-three years, my son
has returned to his old country —
he's back to sell off
jumbo jets, in this recession

even now, in my mind's eye
the vivid image of Toyama-ga-hara
and a child
taking her younger brother
to fly a kite on that field

幼き声

年かけて
戦ひとりしは
同胞の
無数の徒死と
刻々の飢か　　　　　　　　　（カンボジア）

水張りて
植附けを待つ
峡田より
一斉に揚がる
蟇の太声

わが庭に
一つ棲みつきし
蟇蛙の
いまだ幼く
二つ三つ四つ

形見として歌集を編む

我が詠める
短歌は次元
異なれる
世の呟きと
子孫ら思はん

May Yen Ting

Young Voices

is this what was gained

from years of fighting:

untold numbers of

fellow countrymen killed in vain,

starvation from time to time?   (Cambodia)

the expanse of water

awaits its planting—

from valley paddies

all at once a great chorus

of loud-voiced toads

a single toad,

still young, came to live

in my garden—

now there are two

or three or four of them

I compile a collection of *tanka* as a keepsake.

they'll probably think

of the tanka *I compose,*

as murmurings

from a different dimension,

my children and grandchildren

Figure 2 – Ting Yen May with husband, Ting Ruey-Iang.

Afterword

I spent two and half years at the Tokyo Prefectural First Girls' High School just before the Great Kantō Earthquake [関東大震災] of 1923. After the earthquake, I studied at the Taipei Provincial First Girls' High School [台北州立第一高女] for a year and a half. I thought of attending the Tokyo Women's Higher Normal College located at Ochanomizu just because I once lived in the vicinity of Hongō Yushima 5-chome area. "Gan-San, it is very difficult to study science. There is no need for a girl to spend such a busy life studying," said my advisor. I changed my major from science to liberal arts on my application form without much thought. Upon reflection, my motivation for entering the college was without serious or deep thought.

During four years of college, my desire for learning was relatively low even though there were many expert professors. Under the pretext of majoring in liberal arts, I pretended to be a person of refined taste and attended all sorts of events and toured everywhere.

As for poetry, Ogami Shibashu-sensei [尾上柴舟先生] assigned some for homework my senior year. Every time, I counted the syllables on my fingers and arranged them to just meet the required format. I vaguely recall I turned in the homework without fail until my graduation.

For a few years following graduation, I had the urge to tell stories through poetry, but this was just a passing thought and nothing really came of it. Later, under the pressure of household chores, raising and educating children and with the passing of years, even the idea of it had faded. In particular, after World War II, anything relating to Japan had ceased to be pertinent. Also, without the existence of international relations, there was no way to learn about the state of Japanese *tanka* after the war.

I had known about *Chō-On* [潮音] while attending Tokyo Women's Higher Normal College. I also learned that Ōta-sensei, who had taught us Japanese (the national language) in our first year at Tokyo Prefectural First Girls' High School, was actually Shiga Mitsuko-sensei. It warms my heart just to think about this relationship.

More than ten years ago, I came across a Japanese newspaper by chance and discovered that Shiga-sensei was one of the nominees for the *Tanka* Festival held at the [Emperor's] Palace. Soon after, I saw the enlarged photo of Shiga-sensei on the Japan Weekly Graph [日本週刊グラフ]. From that moment, I began wondering if there might be the possibility of meeting her once again or communicating with her by mail.

Four years ago, I unexpectedly received a letter from Moritomo Toshiko-sama [森友とし子様], one of my classmates at Tokyo Prefectural First Girls' High School. She informed me that she had been studying *tanka* under Shiga-sensei's guidance for some time. I was very envious of her and felt Shiga-sensei's presence very close to me.

In May 1971, on the way to the United States, I met Moritomo-sama in Tokyo. She presented me with her precious *Works of* Tanka *of Shiga Mitsuko* [四賀光子全歌集]. In July of the same year, on my way home to Taiwan, Uematsu Setsuko-sama [植松節子様] gave me her book, *Heart of Going, Heart of Returning* [行く心帰る心]. I further learned that Shiga-sensei was an aunt of Setsuko-sama's. I was pleasantly surprised by all these coincidental and unexplainable connections. The pleasure of these discoveries transformed into my determination to write *tanka* and led to a phone call to Shiga-sensei.

As if it were chasing after me, soon after returning to Taiwan, I received a letter from Shiga-sensei indicating that she was anxious to read my *tanka*. With her generous encouragement, and despite my inexperience, I initially wrote ten poems as a trial.

Taking the attitude that diligence could compensate my lack of ability,

274

I learned from Seikyū-sensei's monthly cover message and guidance, and occasionally I encouraged myself by recalling the tale of Idogawa-sama [井戸川様] that a collection of small streams would gradually combine into a larger flow [of water]. I simply devoted myself to follow Shiga-sensei's lead and teachings. Thus I have stayed with it, and now it has been three and a half years since I started writing *tanka*.

Shiga-sensei often advised me that I should save my work and leave them for my children. I often felt very embarrassed just to think of my imperfect works. She also mentioned the works would be a keepsake from me. I interpreted with my own sense that there would be no need to judge if they were good or bad if they were to be a keepsake. My age was also a factor that pushed my will to move forward.

On this matter, Shiga-sensei advised me to get the works ready early. She said to copy down all the written *tanka* and offered to review the draft for me.

I am grateful that Shiga-sensei, at the age of ninety, offered to spend her precious time on me. I felt I was such a fortunate person, and I cannot thank her enough.

The purpose of this afterword is to explain how my imperfect *tanka* came about, and even though they are still not mature, they are to be published.

I would like to express my great appreciation from the bottom of my heart to Shiga-sensei for her guidance and teaching.

Ting Yen May
March 3, 1975

Destiny

About the Author

Ting Yen May was born in Taiwan during the Japanese Occupation. At the age of eleven, she was sent to Tokyo for schooling. She overcame her language deficiencies and successfully completed high school in Japan and became the first Taiwanese to graduate from Ochanomizu University. She learned Mandarin Chinese after the end of World War II and the end of the Japanese Occupaton. In her late fifties, she taught Japanese at Tatung College of Technology [大同工學院] and wrote several Japanese language textbooks. She began writing Japanese poetry (*tanka*) in her sixties after reconnecting with her high school teacher/mentor who guided and encouraged her in publishing *Destiny*, her first book of *tanka*. *Two Countries* is her second collection of *tanka*. Ting Yen May's creative ability and perseverance in overcoming every obstacle led to her success in life.

About the Translator

Amelia Fielden, an Australian, is a professional translator of Japanese literature, specializing in the translation of *tanka* poetry. She is also an internationally published and awarded poet writing tanka in English.

Amelia gained a Bachelor of Asian Studies (Japanese Honors) degree from the Australian National University and holds a post-graduate diploma in Modern Japanese Translation and a Master of Arts (Japanese Literature).

Over the last twenty years, 24 books of Amelia's *tanka* translations have been published. These include work by poet Kawano Yuko, English collaborations with other poets, bilingual *tanka* anthologies, and her own original poetry, the latest being 'These Purple Years.'

Amelia is an active member of the Limestone Poets (Australia), The Tanka Society of America, and the International Tanka Society.

www.ingramcontent.com/pod-product-compliance
Lightning Source LLC
Chambersburg PA
CBHW060007100426
42740CB00010B/1422